COLORING MANDALAS 1

For Insight, Healing, and Self-Expression

SUSANNE F. FINCHER

SHAMBHALA

Boston & London

2000

Shambhala Publications, Inc.
Horticultural Hall
300 Massachusetts Avenue
Boston, Massachusetts 02115
www.shambhala.com

For information on Susanne Fincher's workshops, books, and tapes, please see her web page at *www.creatingmandalas.com* or contact her at:

The Psychotherapy Group
1551 Jennings Mill Road
Bldg. 2500A
Bogart, Georgia 30622
(706) 369-0697
sfincher@mindspring.com

16 15 14 13 12 11 10 9 8 7

Printed in Malaysia

⊛ This edition is printed on acid-free paper that meets the American National Standards Institute z39.48 Standard.

Distributed in the United States by Random House, Inc., and in Canada by Random House of Canada Ltd

Designed by Dede Cummings Designs

Library of Congress Cataloging-in-Publication Data
Fincher, Susanne F., 1941–
Coloring mandalas: for insight, healing, and self-expression/Susanne F. Fincher.—1st ed.
p. cm.
Includes bibliographical references.
ISBN 1–57062–583–2 (alk. paper)
1. Mandala. 2. Coloring books. I. Title
BL604.M36F557   2000
291.3'7—dc21
99–058715

Entering the Circle

CREATING a mandala begins with drawing a circle. It can be as simple as the circle a child draws or as complex as the sacred images created by Tibetan monks (plate 1). Mandalas arise from the compelling human need to know our own inner reality, to align this knowing with our body's wisdom, and to awaken in ourselves a sense of being in harmony with the universe. As Lama Nubpa Chodak Gyatso has explained, mandalas are "manifestations of the lucid radiance of being." The word *mandala*, from Sanskrit, the ancient language of India, translates as "sacred circle." In Tibetan the term for mandala is *kyil-kor*, which means "center and circumference." In the Eastern tradition mandalas also suggest a complete cycle, such as the rituals that comprise a liturgical year.

Imagine standing on a beach and turning in place. If you touch a stick to the sand, you can easily mark off a circle. Notice how the circle you draw organizes empty space into pairs of opposites: inside/outside, here/there, and near/far. The power of the circle to establish order takes on sacred meaning in an Egyptian myth of creation:

Before the beginning of time, the Uroboros, a great snakelike dragon, floats in the formless void. In this place that is no place, everything swirls together, entangled in confusion. All is gray because dark is intermingled with light. There is nothing to drink because water is buried in dry earth. There is no comfort because softness is laced with prickling sharpness.

Moving within this muddle, the Uroboros slowly, majestically arches back and bites its own tail, thus creating a circle. As the myth relates, with this act, primordial chaos is transformed. The circle formed by the Uroboros sets in motion the separation of the opposites. Light emerges from darkness, water flows away from dry earth, and the touch of softness can soothe because it is freed from hardness. All is put in order, with each having its own time and place to be.

Making a circle always brings order to things. Order begets patterns that the mind can grasp and understand. Even chaotic scribbling achieves a certain harmony when enclosed in a circle. Each time you turn a circle or color a mandala, you invite a little harmony into your life. Arranging forms and colors in a circular design is like the act of the Uroboros, separating confusion into patterns of meaning.

Here is something else to know about circles. A circle suggests a center point in much the same way a magnifying glass acts to focus the sun's rays to a single, bright spot. In a circle the center is always present, and it attracts your eye, whether it is marked or not. The capacity of the circle to catch and focus your attention means that you take less notice of what is outside the circle. As meditators know, concentrating your attention on one thing produces a general relaxation in your body: your breath deepens, your heartbeat slows. These physiological changes release your body's natural healing processes. Traditional healers intuitively make use of mandalas because their circular form organizes perception, thought, and physical responses in ways that are beneficial.

Circles are not just an invention of human beings. Circular forms abound in the natural world. When you toss a pebble into still water, you see a gentle pulsing of circles outward from the point of impact. The harmless dust devils that sweep across a summer picnic whirl around and around as they ruffle napkins and drop bits of this and that. Flowers, rocks, caves, and mountains seen from above suggest the form of the circle (see plate 2). The shining circular form of the moon illuminates the night sky, while the sun's radiant disk lights up the day.

The experiences of countless generations of people with these natural circles have been handed down to us in layer upon rich layer of meaning associated with the circle. Circles represent something with no beginning and no end, something eternal. Circles remind us of the familiar, as in a family circle or a circle of friends. Largely because of the regular movements of the sun and the moon, circles have come to signify cycles of time, the seasons, and the yearly renewal of plant and animal life. The impressive forms of the sun and moon have even served as natural symbols, helping human beings organize their thoughts about mysteries such as life and death.

We can see how this might have happened when we consider the moon. In a month's time, the moon presents a graphic display of a silver disk coming into being, shining in fullness, gradually disappearing, and then appearing once again. Witnessing the coming and going of the moon, month after month, year after year, it is easy to see how changes in the moon helped shape our ancestors' thoughts as they grappled with the mystery of human life. The human life span from childhood to adulthood is aptly illustrated by the waxing of the moon. The full moon's waning to darkness tracks the process of aging, ending in death. The return of the moon following total darkness has naturally given rise to ideas of reincarnation among some peoples. The very earliest mandalas carved in rocks from South Africa to Scandinavia seem to express thoughts about the mystery of life symbolized by the changes observed in the moon, the sun, and the seasons.

Ancient peoples observed the presence of circles in their own bodies, and they especially associated circles with the mystery of birth. In a room thought to be the birthing chamber in a Cretan palace, circles with a single dot in the center decorate the walls (see mandala 14). Archeologists suggest these circles represent the cervix, the circular muscle through which a baby passes when it is born.

We now know that circles are important at every stage of human development. You begin life as a tiny spherical egg enfolded in the snug circular space of your mother's womb. Typically, you leave the womb through your mother's birth canal. Just before birth, your head presses against her cervix to widen the opening. In this moment, called "crowning," you produce your first mandala: the soft top of your head framed by the circular opening of your mother's body. And then you move on through the circle and you are born into the world.

The eyes through which you view your world are round. They are equipped with a circular iris and pupil, so that you literally take in all visual information through structures that are round. Your visual field, the sum total of what you can see, is roughly circular as well, and the point of clearest focus is at the center of your visual field. As you will notice, vision becomes less and less clear away from this focal center, and fades to darkness at the edge of the visual field. Your field of vision is a sort of mandala: a circular area with a center focus.

It seems that your original sense of self can be formed with the information available to you in your circular field of vision. Using nothing more than what it can see as it looks down at its own body, an infant can construct a rudimentary sense of self as "that which is always present." It is thought that more sophisticated notions of self-identity are rooted in this fundamental impression of self. This original sense of self may well be recalled or reinforced when focusing on a circle later in life. This could help explain the sense of peace reported by people when they are painting or drawing within the circular form of the mandala.

Nature has seen to it that babies are programmed to seek out circles. Researchers have found that infants show a preference for rounded shapes and the curved edges of faces almost from birth. This has survival value because it helps a baby find its mother's round breast and get the nourishment it needs. The natural urge for caregiver and infant to gaze into each other's face builds an emotional bond that helps babies to thrive. Your early experiences with nurturing influence your feelings about circles—and mandalas—even as an adult.

Children's Drawing

Children's drawing evolves as the child's physical, emotional, and cognitive abilities develop. Children begin random scribbling around age two. By the age of three, you can observe circles appearing in the scribbles. Shortly after this, children are able to draw circles when they choose, without scribbling. Then they begin to give meaning to their circles.

I remember a family art therapy session where a three-year-old girl sat on her brother's lap, looking at magazines. Page after page, she pointed to the infants she saw and exclaimed, "Baby!" After a while she took a piece of paper and drew a circle. "Baby," she declared with delight, pointing to the circle she had drawn. Clearly, for her the circle represented a little person, like the infants she had seen in the magazines. It probably represented her dawning awareness of herself as such a little person.

After mastering the drawing of circles, children discover how to add lines to their circles. Without any in-

FIGURE 1
The mandala of a three-year-old girl is a likeness of her father.

FIGURE 2
Children's mandalas (top row) *resemble ancient rock carvings* (bottom row).

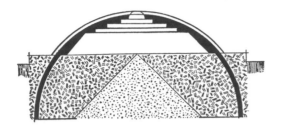

FIGURE 3
*Borobudur temple elevation and ground plan,
illustrating the mandala pattern.*

struction from adults, they spontaneously begin to create mandalas: suns, radial designs, faces, and people (figure 1). Their designs are very like those left by ancient peoples in cave paintings and rock carvings (figure 2). Interestingly, children's mandala drawings coincide with their discovery of themselves as individuals. As they draw mandalas, children become aware of themselves as unique, separate beings, capable of willed action. For children all over the world, drawing mandalas is an integral part of the natural development of self-consciousness.

Mandalas as Sacred Art

Visionaries of the East represent their spiritual insights in complex mandalas based on the form of the circle (plates 1 and 3). These mandalas are considered sacred and are used to help devotees increase their understanding of nonra-

tional realities. Some mandalas are thought to hold healing powers. Creating mandalas as a meditation is prescribed for illness, for clearing blocks to spiritual enlightenment, or even for gaining favor from a local deity. So it is that women in rural villages of India sweep their front yards clean each morning and mark off a mandala with colored rice powder to invite the blessings of the Goddess on themselves and their families.

Permanent mandalas in the form of sacred architecture are also created to mark special places and serve as a focal point for rituals of devotion. For example, the Buddhist temple at Borobudur in Indonesia consists of eight ascending platforms, surmounted by a large circular dome (figure 3). There are approaches to the central dome from each of the four directions. The whole structure is a symbolic model of the universe. Ritual movements in and around the site act out the journey toward enlightenment.

At Sanchi, in India, throngs of pilgrims visit a similar structure marking the place of Buddha's enlightenment. Pilgrims enter a square enclosure through a gate in the east. They mount steps to a platform and circle the dome in a clockwise direction, extending their right hands toward the center. In rituals like those performed at Borobudur and Sanchi, you enter and become one with the mandala of the shrine, and by doing so you integrate into your own being the ideal harmony embodied in the site.

Tibetan Buddhist monks create mandalas that are considered a dwelling place for a deity, and they often depict a bird's-eye view of a structure like the ones at Sanchi and Borobudur (figure 4). It can generally be said that Tibetan mandalas are created with the intention of inviting, containing, honoring, and integrating certain kinds of energy exemplified in gods and deities. Every element in the mandala has symbolic meaning. These mandalas provide a visual form of instruction about spiritual truths.

Traditional meditation practices prescribe the order in which attention is directed to each part of the mandala. The line followed by the gaze of meditators is very like the path taken by pilgrims walking through sacred mandala sites like those at Sanchi and Borobudur. Creating and meditating on such mandalas helps the Buddhist discover a way into and out of deep states of mental concentration. The mandalas guide meditators to a realization of them-

FIGURE 4
Tibetan mandalas resemble the floor plan of a temple.

selves as spiritual and physical beings existing within a harmonious cosmos.

Mandalas are used in similar ways in the traditions of Native Americans. Mandala patterns on pottery pieces tell stories and teach values. For example, the Zuñi story of the pattern called "Cloud All Alone" (mandala 31) emphasizes the importance of participating in communal rituals. The Native Americans of the Pacific Northwest carve dishes and bowls decorated with the forms of totem animals such as bear, raven, and killer whale (mandala 43). These handsome decorative patterns with symbolic meanings may also be considered mandalas.

The medicine wheel is another type of Native American mandala. It is a circle representing the horizon line, divided at four points for each of the four cardinal directions (figure 5). Some versions include additional directions—up, down,

7

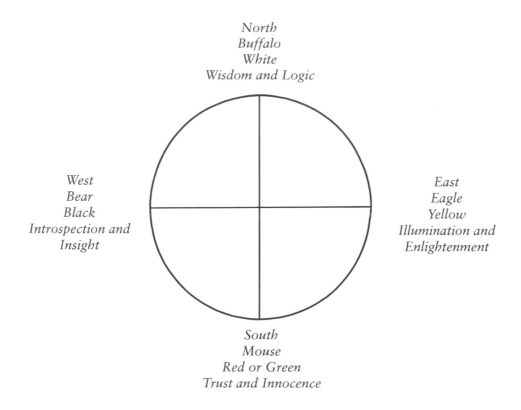

North
Buffalo
White
Wisdom and Logic

West
Bear
Black
Introspection and
Insight

East
Eagle
Yellow
Illumination and
Enlightenment

South
Mouse
Red or Green
Trust and Innocence

FIGURE 5
The Native American medicine wheel has special attributes for each direction.

and center—for a total of seven directions in all. Each of the four cardinal directions has symbolic animals, colors, and other qualities associated with it. Native Americans use the medicine wheel as a way to teach wisdom about the earth, cycles of life, spirituality, and self-knowledge.

Each direction represents a different way of viewing reality. It is thought that you are born into one direction and know it easily. You spend your life learning about the other three. It is necessary to experience, understand, and balance the wisdom of all four directions in order to become a whole person. The mandala of the medicine wheel exemplifies the balance of all four directions.

Mandalas are also important in Native American healing practices. Among the Navahos, when someone is sick, the family calls on a medicine man for help. As part of his healing ceremony he creates a beautiful sand painting in a traditional mandala pattern. The design of the sand painting is selected to correct the disharmony that is thought to

be the cause of illness. The sick person is placed upon the sand painting to correct imbalances. Health returns once harmony is restored.

Mandalas are found also in the traditions of Europe, where mystics have used circular designs as a way to express and share their visions and insights. Hildegard of Bingen, a twelfth-century Benedictine nun, recorded her inspired visions in lovely mandala paintings (mandala 20). The mystic Jakob Boehme used mandalas to express his conviction that God is a unity of both darkness and light. Giordano Bruno, an Italian Renaissance philosopher, created mandala patterns designed to stimulate improvement in the character of those who studied them (mandala 25).

Mandalas are also seen in Christian churches—in such forms as stained-glass window designs and labyrinths—where they may be used for teaching, contemplation, and symbolic pilgrimages. Circular stained-glass windows, called rose windows, appear in many Gothic cathedrals.

FIGURE 6
Labyrinth in Chartres Cathedral.

Like all mandalas, they engage attention and bring it to the center, which is reserved for holy images. For example, the rose window of Nôtre Dame Cathedral in Paris depicts the Virgin and Child in the center, surrounded by figures of biblical prophets, kings, and patriarchs.

The labyrinth, a meandering path to a center point, is also a mandala. Labyrinths are found in medieval Christian churches, worked into the floor so that they can be walked on. The center in a Christian labyrinth is often occupied by a mystic rose, thought to symbolize the Holy Spirit and the process of spirit coming into matter. The beautiful labyrinth in Chartres Cathedral (figure 6) served medieval Christians as a metaphorical pilgrimage. It has recently been rediscovered by modern pilgrims who use it as a walking meditation that supports a personal experience of the Christ within.

Jung on Mandalas

C. G. Jung introduced modern Westerners to the psychological significance of mandalas. He believed that we all have the urge to fulfill our own unique pattern, to live out our potential, to experience wholeness. At the very core of the personality, not directly accessible to consciousness, lies the true center of the psyche, which Jung called the Self. The Self functions both as your potential for wholeness and as the energizing force that nudges you toward fulfilling your possibilities. The Self to which we relate in our psyches is not, strictly speaking, "ours," because it transcends the personal. You might think of it as a spark of the life force that dwells everywhere in all things. Like a holo-

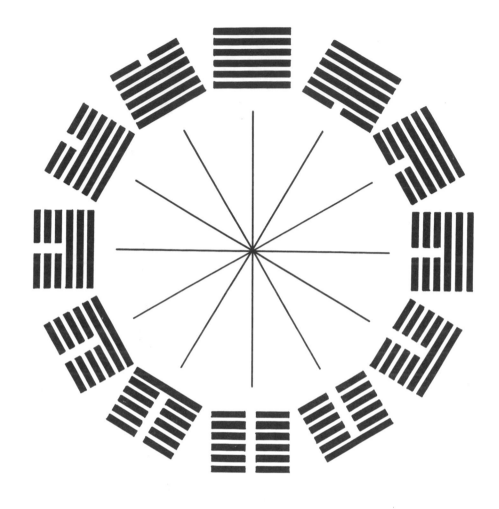

FIGURE 7
Twelve hexagrams of the I Ching *show the alternating rhythm of* yin *(feminine, receptive, broken lines) and* yang *(masculine, active, unbroken lines).*

graphic image, it brings into your psyche a perfect and complete image of all creation, including your own individual existence. For some, the communications of the Self are experienced as the voice of God within, offering timeless wisdom and spiritual understanding. Mandalas symbolize this pattern of wholeness in each of us.

The Self is the true center of personality. The most familiar part of your personality, that which you call "I," Jung referred to as the "ego." Your ego and Self are in a dynamic relationship throughout your life. The Self exists from the beginning of life. Your ego, on the other hand, comes into existence during early childhood. It arises from the matrix of the Self something like the way an island is formed when natural forces push land above the ocean.

Your ego and Self communicate in an ongoing dialogue that allows the unconscious pattern of wholeness to come into being through your ego. When your ego is too small, too large, or otherwise blocks fulfillment of your pattern of wholeness, difficulties arise. The Self may even challenge or disrupt your ego functioning in order to nudge you toward wholeness. At the end of life, when individual existence ceases, the ego dissolves once again into the Self.

Mandalas Communicate

The mandalas you draw or color communicate information between the Self and your ego. The forms and colors in mandalas are symbolic. They convey meaning visually, without words. Mandalas translate information from your ego into symbolic language that communicates to the Self. Creating mandalas reflects your inner experience in artwork so that you can then study, understand, and integrate the messages from the unconscious.

Inner conflicts naturally arise as you grow and change. For example, a message from the unconscious to become more emotionally expressive may be experienced by your ego as a threatening loss of control. When the conflict between these opposing viewpoints—"impulsive emotional expression" versus "controlled emotion"—is fully experienced, a third point of view will emerge from the unconscious that transcends the conflict and brings both viewpoints into a completely new and harmonious synthesis. This bridging viewpoint facilitates "appropriate emotional expression"—that is, greater ease of emotional expression within the bounds of social acceptability. The Self is the source of the breakthrough that resolves conflict, and it is not unusual for solutions to come in the form of spontaneous mandalas that are dreamed, drawn, colored, or danced. Thus, working with mandalas becomes a way to actively support the inner conversation between Self and ego.

The relationship between ego and Self follows a natural cycle of active engagement, distancing, and dormancy followed by reengagement. Many have found similarities between the flux and flow in human lives and the Great Round of the growing year of plants. Other models for life have been found in the stately passages of sun, moon, and stars. A Chinese concept of this circle-dance of life is found in the I Ching, where dark, receptive yin energies alternate with light, active yang energies (figure 7).

Even before these systems of thought were devised, the ever-turning wheel of the year gave order and symmetry to human life. In many cultures it was customary to divide the year into twelve months (originally "moonths"). Each month has its own activities associated with the cultivation of crops, the tending of animals, and the production of food. Just as the division of the year into months helps us to think about the whole year, envisioning a complete cycle in twelve stages can be a helpful way of conceptualizing the relationship between your ego and the Self.

The Great Round of the Psyche

Variations in the connection between your ego and the Self create a cyclical rhythm in your psychological life and your body's physical existence. This rhythm is experienced in alternating periods of activity and quiescence. When your ego is closely aligned with the Self, you tend to feel energetic, confident, and outgoing. When the relationship between your ego and Self is disrupted or in transition, you naturally feel less sure of yourself, have less energy, and tend to be more introspective. Your sense of this ongoing process, the Great Round of the psyche, is of a continuous stream of consciousness and activity. For purposes of understanding, it can be helpful to identify twelve distinctive stages in this continuum.

Consider that each of the twelve stages of the Great Round is a distinct aspect of your ego experience. Each has a characteristic point of view, its own special strengths, and its own challenges. If you envision these twelve stages as arranged in a circle, then the Self occupies the center of the circle. Just as the ego arises from the Self, the twelve stages of ego-experience that comprise the Great Round have their source in the Self, the center and ground of your being. The beginning and ending point of your ego's cycling through the twelve stages is a resting place in the Self that is beyond the dualities of ordinary existence (the American art therapist Joan Kellogg calls this experience stage 0, "Clear Light.") As your ego cycles through the twelve stages, you learn more about the center and source of your being, and the relationship between your ego and the Self evolves. With each complete cycle, you explore a different level of meaning.

The initial circulation of the Great Round coincides with your physical development and maturation for most stages. Subsequent passages focus on refinements in psychosocial development. Each time you visit a stage, you have an opportunity to deepen, expand, or rework your ego structure. Eventually, the circulation of the Great Round becomes a way to explore and develop your spirituality. The ultimate realization of the Great Round is awareness of the Center, the Self, and the stages of your ego experience as a whole in perfect balance and harmony: a mandala.

The Twelve Stages of the Great Round

As with the four directions of the Native American medicine wheel, each stage of the Great Round has a particular point of view, highlights certain abilities, and presents challenges to be confronted in order to assimilate the lessons of that stage. Stages near the beginning are characterized by dreamy, unfocused energy that recalls experiences of early life. In the middle of the cycle, one is most productive. Equally important are the stages near the end of the cycle when energy withdraws from your ego into the unconscious as the Self directs deep restructuring of your ego. Now let us explore in a little more detail what each stage is like.

Stage 0 (zero), Clear Light, is experienced prior to self-awareness. It consists of the quality of sentience, of pure consciousness that is the ground of being, the cradle of all existence. Clear Light is our own portion of the consciousness that animates all the universe. It is the Self, the matrix within which our ego forms.

We may not often experience the state of pure consciousness, yet a capacity for consciousness is the basis for all ego experiences. An ongoing connection with its original source, Clear Light, gives our ego vitality. Awareness of the importance of Clear Light comes only with the ability of our ego to see itself and its stages as rooted in this primal Center of existence. Clear Light is a dimension outside of space and time, where we begin life and where we return once our individual existence is fulfilled.

Stage 1, the Void, is a viewpoint that is first developed during the intrauterine experience prior to birth. There is no sense of individual will here. Time seems to stand still in an eternal Now. You may experience physical sensations of pressure, heaviness, or claustrophobia that could recall your birth experience. This stage can be triggered later in life as the aftermath of sweeping changes to your sense of who you are. It may also follow extreme physical challenges and profound spiritual experiences.

In Stage 1, the Void, your ego is closely aligned with the Self in a covert, paradoxical relationship called negative inflation. This gives you an exaggerated sense of yourself as small, powerless, and acted on by external forces. This is a stage when your ego does not function well, and you need to be patient with yourself and put your trust in tried and true instincts to see you through. In terms of spiritual experience, this stage is comparable to the mystic's intense absorption in deep inner states of no-thingness.

Stage 2, Bliss, occurs following birth when, if all goes well, you are cuddled, fed, and cared for in ways that make the world seem a safe and welcoming place. A pleasant lack of ego boundaries characterizes Bliss, even when experienced later in life. This stage is accompanied by deep relaxation. The state of mind is dreamy, drowsy. It has been found that creative persons return to this stage often between periods of productivity, to rest and receive inspiration from the unconscious. Mystics swim in this state of mind as in an ocean of love.

Stage 3, Labyrinth, is developed during an infant's exploration of its body and its surroundings. During the stage of the Labyrinth, an infant experiments with sensing and movement and begins to organize its findings into a map of reality. When experienced later in life, this stage brings flexibility and openness to new information that can be beneficial for healing physical and psychological injuries. Some spiritual practices cultivate this state of consciousness for communicating with the ancestors, for contacting animal spirit guides, or for other shamanic practices. Active searching and exploring, even though not goal directed, gives this stage a characteristically energetic quality.

Stage 4, Beginnings, is opened prior to the age of two, when baby and mother enjoy the ultimate experience of mutual bonding. When its needs are met and its mother takes pleasure in mother love, a baby feels content and trusting. Ever after, this stage is characterized by a pleasant sense of containing and nurturing creative energy, though just what will develop is not at all clear. On a spiritual level, this stage is about feeling compassion for others and serving from heartfelt caring.

Stage 5, Target, is established with the baby's intense experience of leaving the womb. It is further developed during the toddler's discovery of itself as a separate person. Around age two, you begin to actively go after what you want instead of passively waiting for it to be provided, and this creates inevitable conflicts with caregivers. When you do not get what you want, you become frustrated. Not getting your way can even lead to a feeling of being victimized.

During Stage 5, Target, behaviors for self-soothing and protection arise as a normal reaction to feelings of disappointment and vulnerability. These behaviors further define your psychological separateness from others and act to reinforce your ego. Later in life, ritualized behaviors for self-care and self-protection may be elaborated as reassurance that your ego boundaries are adequate. The Target state of mind can be triggered when you feel tired or vulnerable, or when you encounter unexpected resistance from others. On a spiritual level, this stage may bring an appreciation for religious rituals, as well as a realization of the limits imposed by your ego. Considering the possibility of transcending these limits may also occur.

Stage 6, Dragon Fight, has to do with adolescent conflicts that accomplish your separation from your parents, and from the tribe or community in which you grew up. At this stage you may break out of hidebound traditions in general. Dragon Fight is characterized by an increase of tension at all levels of the psyche. Issues are polarized and may be acted out in emotional confrontations with others.

All this conflict creates greater and greater energy until finally enough energy is available to generate a new psychological perspective. The new viewpoint resolves the conflicts between your ego and traditional sources of control into a new synthesis that fully incorporates both sides of the conflict. Important transitions later in life—times such as midlife—can bring you around again to the stage of Dragon Fight. On a spiritual level, this stage is concerned with confronting self-doubt, facing the temptations to misuse power, and working through the contradictions between religious dogma and your own spiritual experience.

Stage 7, Squaring the Circle, is opened when you can function independently and go to school. It is fully developed in young adulthood when you have completed your education and have the potential to create, but as yet you have accomplished little. Intellectual ability is heightened here. This is a time when you are filled with a sense of power, importance, and mission. Your ego is synchronized with the deeper order of the Self and you receive an injection of energy because of this. To use the energy appropriately, you choose goals that will accomplish more than simple fulfillment of ego desires for wealth, health, and happiness. You find projects worthy of your best efforts, projects that challenge you to grow, create, and care for others. Later in life, completing some kind of training, formal or informal, can bring you to an experience of Squaring the Circle. On a spiritual level, this stage is about dedicating yourself to principles and practices that enhance life for you and others.

Stage 8, Functioning Ego, opens during those moments of generative adult life when you are actively engaged in bringing your ideas and inspirations into reality. You are busy doing, no longer just being. During this stage you are comfortable working within groups or organizations in order to accomplish your personal goals. Conversely, you have the ability to feel comfortable by yourself and to work without supervision to accomplish the goals you believe in. The state of mind of Functioning Ego can be triggered as you become engrossed in accomplishing a challenging task, such as remodeling your house, starting a business, or managing interpersonal issues as a community leader. This stage can be activated as you take initiative to bring an inspiration into reality. On a spiritual level, this stage is about finding ways of sharing your wisdom gently and respectfully with others in ways they can understand.

Stage 9, Crystallization, reflects a time of fulfillment, satisfaction, and completion. This stage is opened by your adult experience of finishing a project or fulfilling an important commitment, such as raising a family. A slowing of creative activity and a sense of harmony, balance, and relaxed enjoyment characterize this stage. Crystallization is a sweet time, a moment of joy, and a pause for delight in the cycle of the Great Round. In later cycles, Crystallization is a time when you achieve mastery of a spiritual practice. You may apply your intellect to help you think through a knotty spiritual dilemma and feel a sense of achievement for having done so.

Stage 10, Gates of Death, begins the natural process of ending the Great Round cycle, in preparation for a new beginning. The influence of the Self can be seen in experiences that open this stage. It often comes in losses or obstructions that challenge you and cause you to question who you think you are. You may find that things that were important no longer hold your interest. Sometimes an event, such as an illness, will forcefully shift you to this stage. In the unfolding of human life this stage coincides with late midlife, al-though it is experienced earlier at important turning points in the relationship between your ego and the Self.

This stage can be a bittersweet parting with what was, or a painful rending from what can no longer be. Energy declines for outward things as more and more of it shifts inward into the unconscious. It is a time when you are asked to let go of life the way it was, but you have no sense yet of what is to come. You feel betwixt and between. You may begin to lose touch with the spirituality that has been an easy and comforting relationship with God.

Stage 11, Fragmentation, continues the entropy begun in Gates of Death. This stage is about challenges to your body, and much more. What began as endings in the outer world continues here as a destructuring of your ego to the point that you may feel like a stranger to yourself. This is all a necessary prelude to a major reorganization of your ego. For many this stage is profoundly disturbing, as they find their belief in the ultimate order of things challenged. It is not unusual to feel dizzy or nauseated when experiencing this stage.

Your understanding of the nature of reality may be changed by what you experience here in Fragmentation. It may seem you have completely lost contact with the Self, but the chaos experienced here is really orchestrated by the Self. The disorganization speeds the letting go that is necessary before your ego can be restructured in a stronger, more complex pattern in keeping with your potential for wholeness. The Spanish mystic Saint John of the Cross knew this stage well. He described it as the Dark Night of the Soul. This stage can bring you intense spiritual experiences.

Stage 12, Transcendent Ecstasy, reflects the blissful experience that follows the struggle of the previous stage. It comes as the result of embracing the limitations of the physical body and stepping beyond into a much larger dimension where spirit permeates and supports everything. In this stage, you experience the freedom of tran-

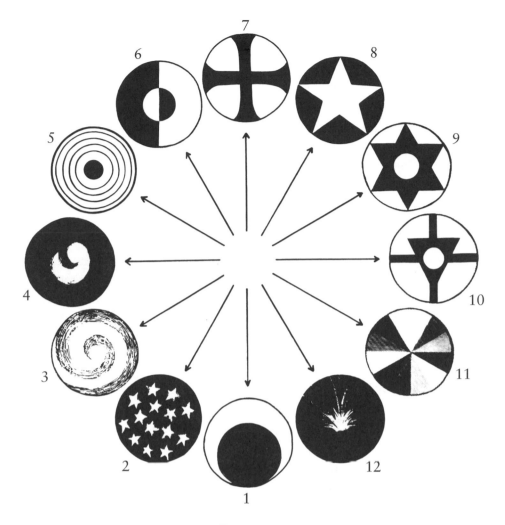

FIGURE 8
Mandala forms of the Great Round (used by permission of Joan Kellogg).

scending beliefs that had become too narrow for you. It is the gift of old age and those rare moments of ecstasy earlier in life. You knowingly surrender your ego to the care of the Self, and you are rewarded with a glimpse of ultimate reality, a sense of the divine order and your rightful place within it.

On a spiritual level, Stage 12, Transcendent Ecstasy, is a moment of understanding the divine through direct experience, rather than by intellect. This is a peak experience. It is a moment to be treasured as the essence of your circling the Great Round. Take it with

you like a seed to be planted in the darkness for your next beginning in Stage 1, the Void.

Mandalas of the Great Round

Joan Kellogg has identified typical mandala forms associated with each of the twelve stages in the Great Round (figure 8). The mandalas in this coloring book are based on the forms identified by Kellogg. There are several mandalas for each of the twelve stages. Mandalas begin with an empty circle, representing Stage 0, Clear Light; continue with

Stage 1, the Void; and go in order through Stage 12, Transcendent Ecstasy.

Coloring the mandalas in this book from beginning to end will be a symbolic visit to each stage of the Great Round. It will take you through every step in a complete cycle of change. As you respond to the mandala forms and add color to them, you will gain insights about each stage in the cycle. And you will discover things about yourself as well. Working with mandalas of stages that are less familiar to you, or where your skills have not been fully developed, can help you extend your experience into new areas. Working with these mandalas of the twelve stages is one way to invite and integrate knowledge from the Self. Looking at the symbolism of the colors you choose, you can learn a lot about your color vocabulary. This will help you unlock the messages from your unconscious that are encoded in the mandalas you color.

Coloring Your Mandalas

We swim in a sea of color. Color is one of life's pleasures. Color communicates information about the world and its creatures. Bees seek out flowers of a certain color for the right kind of nectar. Birds grow fresh, bright plumage in the spring to announce their readiness to reproduce. Ripe fruit can easily be identified by its rich, full color.

Your body responds to color. Color is produced by waves of electromagnetic energy perceived by cells in your eyes, your skin, and even your bones. Reds have the longest wavelengths and transmit the least energy. Violets have the shortest wavelengths and the most energy. In laboratory studies, it has been found that red is stimulating, while blue causes relaxation. Color is simple, direct, and measurable in the natural world.

The physical facts about color are universally true. Whether you are Australian or Portuguese, your measurement of the wavelength of magenta is the same. And your body responds in certain ways to light and color. So it is that an absence of light helps trigger your body's sleep response.

Human beings elaborate on nature's simplicity by assigning complex meanings to color. For example, you have your own personal ideas about what colors mean based on your beliefs, observations, and experiences. In fact, color is a way in to your personal life story. The color you wore on a special occasion will always give your response to that color a particular flavor. Depending on whether that special time was pleasant or unpleasant, your feelings about that color will be positive or negative. Using your personal vocabulary of color meanings, the Self sends you messages in the colors you choose for coloring mandalas.

Colors also take on symbolic meanings in a cultural context. Some meanings have been in use so long that they seem universal. Since we take it for granted that white is the color for brides' dresses, it can be surprising to discover that white is the traditional color of mourning in some Eastern cultures. There, red is the color worn by brides, quite a contrast to our Western tradition of bridal white.

Traditional color meanings in the West are based on seasonal holiday celebrations, religious symbolism, governmental decree, fashion, and even economics. For example, blue is used by Christian iconographers for the robes of the Virgin Mary. Mary is calm, quiet, loving. Her blue robe stimulates a relaxed physical response in keeping with her image. Orange is used for autumn harvest holidays, such as Thanksgiving. The pumpkins harvested at this time are orange, as is the stunning full moon at harvest time. During Roman times purple dye was rare and expensive, so its use was limited to the nobility. Purple has been associated with royalty ever since.

As a way to understand more about the meaning of your colors, here are some steps to follow after you have finished coloring your mandala. List all of the colors you used in your mandala on a sheet of paper. Then, after each color, write down your associations. Just record the words that come to you with as little thought as possible. Then, reading through what you have written, look for patterns of meaning. Your associations give you information about your present state of mind, about the messages from your unconscious, and about what is needed to balance and bring wholeness into your present situation.

Your color associations will draw from each of the levels mentioned: universal (based on your body's physiological responses), personal (growing out of your life experiences), and cultural (defined by custom and tradition). Meanings can be positive or negative. They may overlap or contradict. So, green may stand for pleasant qualities of nature, and it may also be remembered as the color of your room at an enjoyable time in your life. On the other hand, green could also remind you of an overbearing aunt who made a show of her jade jewelry.

Consider that some of your color choices may be a response to the mandala form itself, or the stage it represents. This can give you interesting information about your previous experiences with this stage as well as your present-day feelings about it. Did you choose colors for Bliss, Stage 2, that represent anxiety to you? If so, your mandala may be telling you that your formative experience of this stage during infancy might have been less than secure. For example, you or your mother might have suffered an accident or illness that interrupted your emotional bonding. Knowing this, you can take action to comfort the frightened part of yourself and so reduce your anxiety. Or did you choose colors you love that make you feel happy when coloring mandalas of Stage 8, Functioning Ego? This might suggest you are very comfortable with your creative skills, that you present your ideas to others effectively, and that you feel confident about yourself and your work.

After listing your own associations to colors, refer to the color meanings below for additional information.

Color Meanings

Red, an energizing, stimulating color, relates to the physical body. It increases alertness and brings awareness of the present moment. This color signifies passion, life, sexuality, love, and the power to create. It also symbolizes blood, rage, violence, and fire.

Blue is the color of clear sky, suggesting infinite space, the heavens, and eternity. A calming and relaxing color, it has to do with nurturing aspects of the feminine principle.

Yellow symbolizes the sun and suggests the rhythms of time set in motion by the sun's rising and setting. It has to do with energizing aspects of the masculine principle. Yellow signifies the light of consciousness that has de-

scended into our nervous system to allow us to be self-aware. Yellow relates to emotional energies and for some it represents the soul of a person.

Green is the color of nature, of balance, and of harmony. It represents the primal power of fertility that makes seeds sprout. It is symbolic of freshness, health, peace, and prosperity.

Orange speaks of earthiness, in contrast to spirituality. It stands for the energy of the life force that maintains your body in a healthy balance without your direct attention. The color also represents endurance, strength, and worthy ambition.

Purple relates to nobility, refinement, and power. It signifies patience, trust, faith, and fasting.

Turquoise suggests generosity, love, and healing. Traditional peoples in many parts of the world paint doors and window frames turquoise for protection from dangerous spirits. Turquoise helps maintain safe boundaries.

Brown is a symbol of the earth, of fertility. It is also symbolic of holding or blocking energy.

White refers to the blinding light of the spirit, triumphant over death. White suggests the ashes after a fire, the silence of snow. It is a symbol of purity, innocence, virginity, and birth.

Black suggests the sinister power of darkness, decay, and death. The symbol of mourning, of nonbeing, it also symbolizes protection from evil. It is the color for penitence and respect for the souls of the departed. Remembrance, eternity, and constancy are represented by the color black.

Color Systems

Knowing the way colors work together is helpful when interpreting your mandalas. You will recall the Native American medicine wheel as one system of color. Using this system, you might interpret white in your mandala as related to the direction of North and all it signifies about wis-

FIGURE 9
*Kundalini yoga identifies five chakras along the spine and
two located in the head.*

dom. Yellow is associated with the East, red or green with the South, and black with the West.

The great German poet Goethe formulated a color theory based on his observations and philosophical beliefs. He took white and black to represent opposite poles of existence. White signifies pure light and spirit. Black is symbolic of darkness and matter. Goethe conceptualized all color as differing amounts of light and darkness.

Pure light, as seen in the color white, occupies one end of a color continuum. As light darkens, it produces the color yellow. More darkening creates the color red. At the opposite end of the color continuum, absolute darkness is represented by the color black. When black lightens, it produces the color blue.

Green is the result of mixing equal amounts of blue and yellow. Thus, green represents a halfway point between the opposites black and white. To Goethe, green became symbolic of a desirable state of harmony. It represents a perfect blending of spirit (since yellow is derived from white) and matter (since blue is made by lightening black).

Another system of color meaning is based on the wis-

dom traditions of India. So ancient that its inception precedes recorded history, this system was probably derived from careful introspection. Interestingly enough, contemporary Western psychology has introduced a theory of a hierarchy of human needs not unlike those of Indian thought. Modern healers are coming to appreciate these Indian beliefs as more is learned about the importance of various forms of electrical and magnetic energy in the health of our bodies. To understand the role of color in this theory, let us look briefly at kundalini yoga, the source of these ideas.

The principles of kundalini yoga state that unseen energy flows through certain subtle pathways in your body. Especially important is the flow of energy upward from the base of your spine to the crown of your head. It is thought that along this central channel there are nodal points where energy is concentrated and transformed. These are called *chakras*. There are seven chakras, four spaced several inches apart along your spine, one at your throat, one above and between your eyes, and one at the top of your head (see figure 9).

Each chakra contains certain lessons about life. As

you master these, more energy becomes available to you for living and for learning about other chakras. The ultimate goal is spiritual realization. The lower chakras have to do with survival and basic needs. The upper chakras relate to love, creativity, and spiritual awakening. You cannot fully open the upper spiritual chakras until the lower chakras are fully integrated. You may find yourself returning to a chakra again and again until you have learned the wisdom held there.

Each chakra has a color of the rainbow spectrum associated with it: red, orange, yellow, green, blue, indigo, and purple or lavender. When you use these colors in your mandala, you might want to consider whether you are concerned with the issues of the chakras associated with those colors.

When working with energies of the first chakra, whose color is red, your concerns relate to the physical health of your body, to your needs for basic safety, security, and survival. It suggests that you are engaged in learning about the physical world. Think of a baby's bright red face as it communicates its hunger for all to hear. When red occurs in your mandala, consider whether some part of you is feeling vulnerable or in need of healing. Red may also signify the stirring of energy needed to create something new.

The second chakra is located between your navel and your tailbone, where the reproductive organs are. Its color is orange. This chakra relates to the development of autonomy. Your sense of self-worth, your observations about the effectiveness of your actions, and issues related to gender and sexuality are some of the lessons explored around the second chakra. These concerns emerge in relationships where we learn to act with integrity, honoring our own needs as well as those of the person to whom we have made commitments. The appearance of orange in your mandalas may reveal a connection to earthiness, feelings of joy, and the energy to take action.

The third chakra is located behind the navel in the area of the solar plexus. Its color is yellow. Jung describes this as "the place where the sun rises," meaning that it is associated with the emergence of your ego. Here, you view everything from the point of reference you call "I." The issues here relate to independence, to self-esteem, to your ability to know what you want and how to take ap-

propriate action to get it. Yellow in your mandalas may reveal a readiness to learn, to think, to plan. It may reflect full acceptance of yourself and the development of your own unique point of view.

The fourth chakra, green in color, is located near the heart and has to do with loving. Issues here include the relinquishment of attachment to your parents, the ability to nurture yourself and others, and your readiness for an intimate relationship. Green in your mandalas may announce that you are coming into your own, that you are opening to emotional relatedness with another, or that you are expanding your capacity to love and nurture. Green may show your readiness to forgive, to forgo the debt owed you by someone.

The fifth chakra is in your throat area. Blue is associated with this chakra. It is concerned with creating and communicating in your own voice. This chakra relates to increasing spiritual awareness that allows you to share your gifts, talents, and abilities as an expression of the divine within you, rather than as a way of getting approval for yourself. In the yoga tradition, it is thought to be the gateway to the upper chakras where the individual soul becomes reunited with the larger self, the Atman. Blue in your mandalas may suggest that this is a time for speaking up, for offering your special gifts to the world, and for the awakening of your spiritual nature.

Spiritual awareness deepens even more at the sixth chakra, found just above and between the eyes. The color is dark blue or indigo. This chakra is also known as the third eye, and it relates to your developing wisdom. This chakra is the center for creative visualization, and through this chakra you receive information from your higher self. The challenge of this chakra is to accept your ability to see beyond what is on the surface of a situation and to question and continue to seek the truth. When dark blue appears in your mandalas, consider whether your intuitive abilities are being expanded. Perhaps you are awakening to deeper spiritual understanding, or seeing the Mystery shining through ordinary events in your life.

The seventh chakra crowns the top of your head. The color is purple or lavender. In yoga tradition it is called "the thousand-petaled lotus" and is associated with an ability to transcend your separate existence and to merge into a mystical connection with the cosmos. The lesson here is that you are more than your physical body. The laws of time and place do not bind part of you, and living fully in the present moment is a true expression of this wisdom. Purple or lavender in your mandalas may point toward your realization of wisdom and may be associated with a peak experience or a direct encounter with the divine.

(For more information on colors and forms in mandalas see my book *Creating Mandalas*).

Ways to Use This Book

The first mandala in this book is an empty circle. As a way to begin your mandala work, you may find it helpful to place this image in front of you in order to meditate on what the circle means to you. Does it symbolize openness? Emptiness? Is it inviting? Does the circle speak of fullness? Of safety? Or of limits? Are there qualities you want to invite into yourself, your own circle of being, through this mandala work? Focusing your thoughts in this way each time you begin can help you deepen your work and make a connection to the form of the mandala you are coloring.

Remember this: there are no right or wrong ways to color your mandalas. You may prefer going from front to back, coloring each mandala as you go. Working through the book in order takes you symbolically through a complete cycle of the Great Round and can give you a satisfying sense of completion. The word *mandala* also translates as "cycle," as in a prayer cycle or a song cycle built around a single theme. Coloring all the mandalas outlined in this book is, in itself, creating a mandala.

Another interesting approach might be to work with stage 1 mandalas in January, stage 2 mandalas in February, and so on, so that the coloring book becomes the basis of ongoing creative work throughout the year. You may feel a connection to the natural cycles of the earth when you bring a deeper awareness of the turning of the year to your mandala work. Your mandala coloring could become part of individual or group rituals that acknowledge the cycles of nature and honor your place in the larger rhythms of life.

No doubt you will find some mandalas more interesting than others, and this sets up another way to use this book. In following your personal taste as a guide for working through the book, you can also gain insight into yourself. The mandalas you like will probably reflect the stages in which you are most comfortable. The mandalas that you find dull or distasteful may show you stages that are more difficult for you. Coloring the mandalas you do not like can be an exercise in exploring neglected, forgotten, or undeveloped parts of yourself. Coloring those you like can be a celebration of who you are.

Coloring a mandala is a very personal act. After going deeply within to focus on your work, it can be a pleasure to share what you have done with others. Sharing your mandala and your personal insights with a safe, caring group can give you the added benefit of feedback from others. Remember that what others say indicates more about themselves than it does about you. Still, they may see things that you had not noticed. If you get an "Aha!" feeling listening to what others have to say, there is probably something of value there for you to ponder. When others' observations seem unhelpful or give you an unpleasant feeling, remember that you can choose not to accept what they say as the Truth. No one else can tell you what your mandala means. It is your experience, and you are the final authority on what your mandala is communicating to you.

Some of the mandalas have large, open spaces. Consider these areas an invitation to exercise your creativity by adding your own touches to the design in the book. After working with the mandalas in the book, you will probably want to explore creating your own mandalas. The empty mandala at the beginning of the book can be used as a starting point for your own mandala design.

It can be beneficial to simply color mandalas without any interpretation. This is the approach to use when coloring with children. Adults can nurture a child's self-confidence by refraining from criticism of any kind, by allowing the child to explore coloring mandalas free from guidance about the "proper" way to do it, and by treating the child's mandalas with respect. Then coloring mandalas can be an enjoyable shared activity for both children and adults.

Materials

When selecting materials for coloring mandalas in this book, choose media you like or want to learn more about. The paper will support colored pencils, crayons, chalk, oil pastels, watercolors, tempera paint, or colored inks. The little extra to purchase top-quality art materials will reward you with better results. You might want to explore the possibilities of collage by cutting and gluing colored paper, pictures from magazines, or pieces of cloth onto your mandalas.

Paint and some markers may bleed through the paper, so place a sheet or two of paper underneath your mandala while you work with these media. Paint, ink, and liquid glue will wrinkle the paper a bit, but this can be minimized by placing clean, dry paper towels underneath and on top of your mandala when you are done, closing the coloring book, and resting a book on top until the mandala dries.

Please know that there is no "right" or "wrong" way to go about using this book. Working with mandalas invites the presence of the Self, your psyche's ordering principle. Coloring mandalas brings a sense of calm. The act of focusing on a piece of creative work stimulates the relaxation response, a mental state similar to that of meditation. In this relaxed state, you can shift away from everyday thoughts and concerns in a way that is restful and beneficial for your health.

Coloring mandalas affirms the deepest layers of your personal identity. Mandalas provide a link between your ego and the Self. They help you develop your potential for wholeness. Mandalas serve as a catalyst for group sharing. The mandalas brought into a group act as nonverbal communication that intensifies sharing among group members. Whether done alone or in a group, as an enjoyable activity or as a vehicle for meditation, coloring mandalas is healing. Mandalas lead you into a deeper exploration of your spirituality, help you focus on thoughts that are difficult to put in words, and present new solutions to difficult questions. May it be so for you.

References

Artress, Lauren. *Walking a Sacred Path: Rediscovering the Labyrinth as a Spiritual Tool*. New York: Riverhead Books, 1995.

Boas, Franz. *Primitive Art*. New York: Dover Publications, 1955.

Brauen, Martin. *The Mandala: Sacred Circle in Tibetan Buddhism*. Boston: Shambhala Publications, 1997.

Bremner, Gavin; Slater, Alan; and Butterworth, George (eds.). *Infant Development: Recent Advances*. Hove, East Sussex, U.K.: Psychology Press, 1997.

Brusatin, Manlio. *A History of Colors*. Boston & London: Shambhala Publications, 1991.

Cleary, Thomas (tr. and ed.). *I Ching Mandalas*. Boston & London: Shambhala Publications, 1989.

Cox, Carol Thayer, and Frame, Phyllis. "Profile of the Artist: MARI Card Test Results." *Art Therapy: Journal of the American Art Therapy Association* 10, 1 (1993): 23-29.

Da, Avatara Adi. *The Heart's Shout*. Middleton, Calif.: Dawn Horse Press, 1996.

Edinger, Edward F. *Ego and Archetype*. New York: Viking Penguin, 1987.

Fincher, Susanne F. *Creating Mandalas: For Insight, Healing, and Self-Expression*. Boston & London: Shambhala Publications, 1991.

Fox, Matthew (ed.). *Illuminations of Hildegard of Bingen*. Santa Fe: Bear and Company, 1985.

Gibson, James Jerome. *The Ecological Approach to Visual Perception*. Hillsdale, N.J.: Lawrence Erlbaum Assn., 1986.

Gimbell, Theo. *Book of Color Healing*. London: Gaia Books, 1994.

Gimbutas, Marija. *The Language of the Goddess*. San Francisco: HarperSanFrancisco, 1991.

Goethe, Johann Wolfgang von. *Theory of Colors* (1840). Cambridge: M.I.T. Press, 1970.

Gyatso, Lama Nubpa Chodak. "The Shi-tro Mandala for Universal Peace." *Snow Lion Newsletter* 14, 3 (1999).

Judith, Anodea. *Eastern Body, Western Mind: Psychology and the Chakra System as a Path to the Self*. Berkeley: Celestial Arts, 1996.

Jung, C. G. *Mandala Symbolism*. Princeton, N.J.: Princeton University Press, 1973.

Kagan, Jerome. *The Second Year: The Emergence of Self-Awareness*. Cambridge: Harvard University Press, 1981.

Kellogg, Joan. *Mandala: Path of Beauty*. Rev. ed. Williamsburg, Va.: Privately published, 1997.

Kellogg, Rhoda. *Analyzing Children's Art*. Palo Alto, Calif.: National Press Books, 1970.

Kluckhohn, Clyde, and Leighton, Dorothea. *The Navaho*. Rev. ed. Garden City, N.Y.: Doubleday & Company, 1962.

Kohler, Wolfgang. *Gestalt Psychology*. New York: Liveright, 1992.

Loomis, Mary E. *Dancing the Wheel*. Wilmette, Ill.: Chiron Publications, 1991.

Marks, David F. "On the Relationship between Imagery, Body, and Mind." In *Imagery: Current Developments*, edited by Peter J. Hampson, David F. Marks, and John T. E. Richardson. London: Routledge, 1990.

Shamdasani, Sonu (ed.). *The Psychology of Kundalini Yoga: Notes on the Seminar Given in 1932 by C. G. Jung*. Princeton, N.J.: Princeton University Press, 1996.

Tucci, Giuseppe. *Theory and Practice of the Mandala*. London: Rider and Company, 1961.

Yogananda, Paramahansa. *Autobiography of a Yogi*. Los Angeles: Self-Realization Fellowship, 1987.

Ywahoo, Dhyani. *Voices of Our Ancestors*. Boston & London: Shambhala Publications, 1987.

PLATE I
*This Buddhist mandala on a temple wall in Bhutan depicts
the creation of the cosmos by the circling motion of primal
forces. By this action the elements are spun into existence,
and celestial bodies are set in motion. Twelve astrological circles in the colors of the rainbow plus black and white depict
the orbits of the sun, moon, and stars through the seasons.*
(Photo by Ursula Gansser. Reprinted by permission from The Mystic Art
of Ancient Tibet *by Blanche Olschak ©1973)*

PLATE 2
Flowers are among the many mandala forms in nature.
(Photo by Andrew Fletcher)

PLATE 3
This is a drawing of visions reported by mystics such as Yogananda and Adi Da, in which the essence of existence takes the form of a mandala whose center is a radiant white star, representing the higher levels of cosmic consciousness, on a background of blue, representing subtle planes of manifestation, radiating outward into levels of material manifestation.

PLATE 4
The ever-turning rhythm of the seasons, the Great Round, becomes a pattern for the stages of life as shown in this mandala.
(Used by permission of Peri Aston)

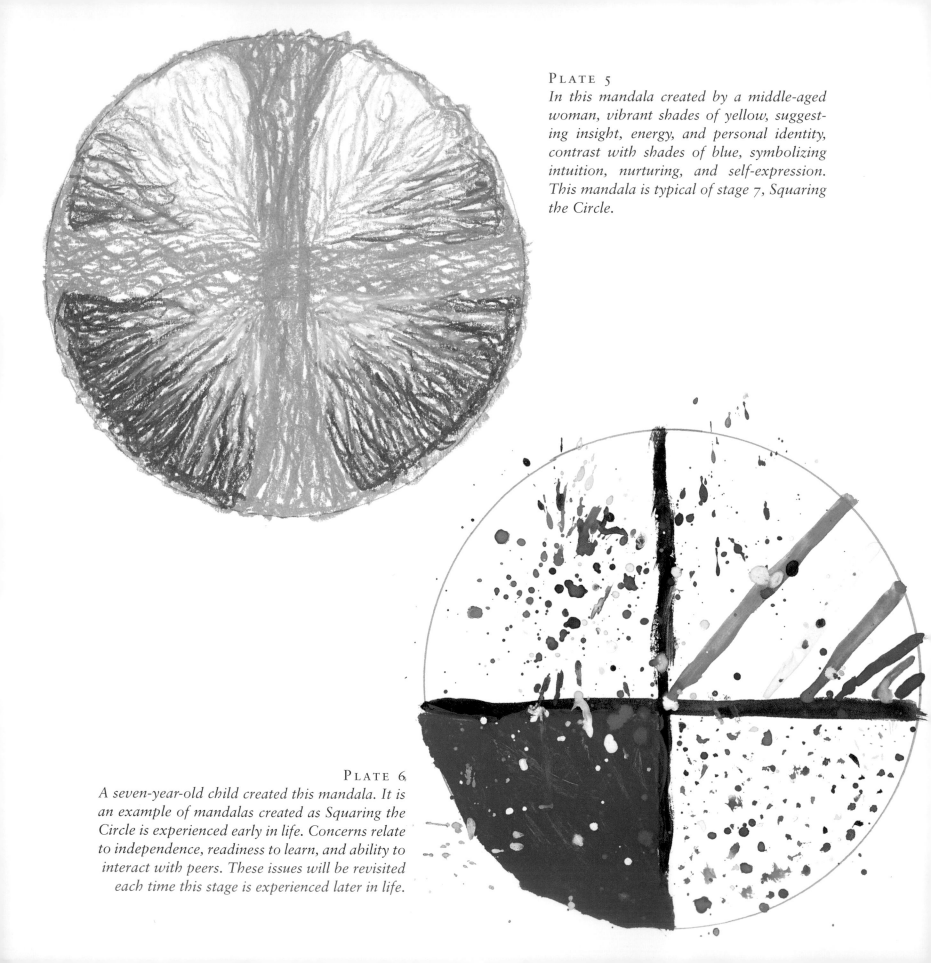

PLATE 5
In this mandala created by a middle-aged woman, vibrant shades of yellow, suggesting insight, energy, and personal identity, contrast with shades of blue, symbolizing intuition, nurturing, and self-expression. This mandala is typical of stage 7, Squaring the Circle.

PLATE 6
A seven-year-old child created this mandala. It is an example of mandalas created as Squaring the Circle is experienced early in life. Concerns relate to independence, readiness to learn, and ability to interact with peers. These issues will be revisited each time this stage is experienced later in life.

PLATE 7
Later in life, stages of the Great Round offer opportunities to deepen spiritual understanding.
This mandala, created by the same woman ten years after the mandala in plate 5, is a more complex design
integrating white (representing light, consciousness, and spirit) into the large central cross form (representing ego).

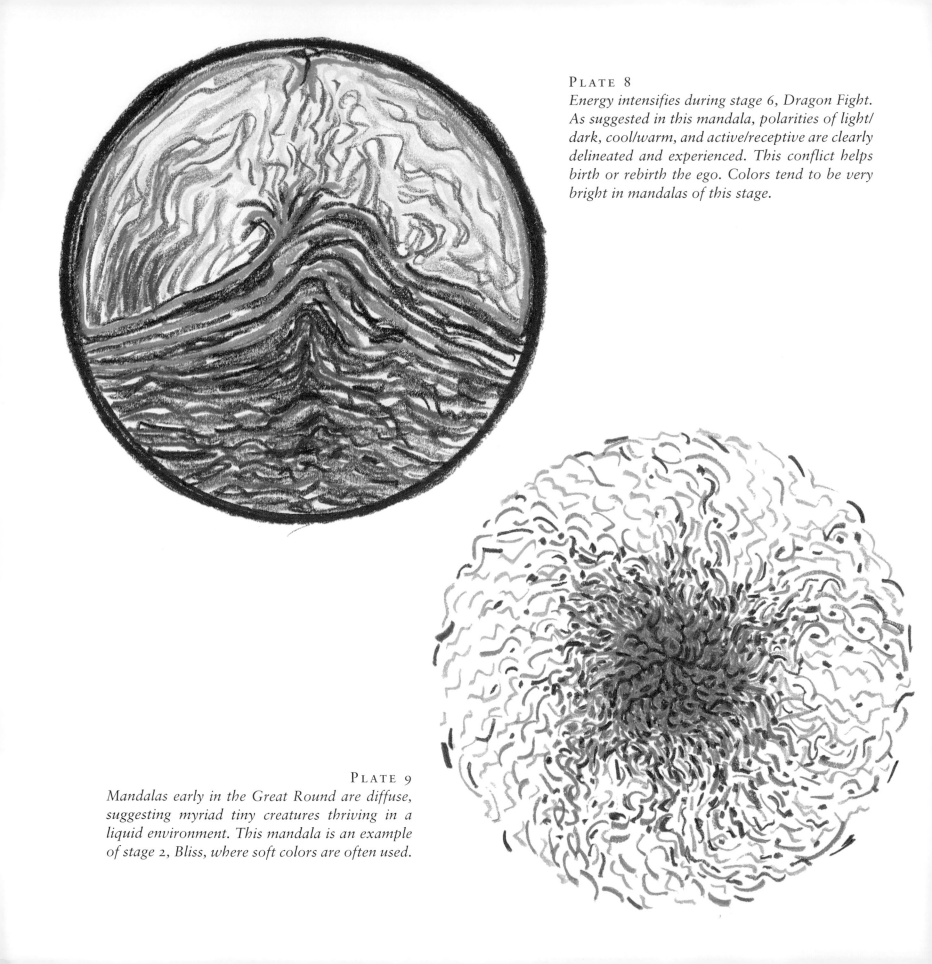

PLATE 8
Energy intensifies during stage 6, Dragon Fight.
As suggested in this mandala, polarities of light/
dark, cool/warm, and active/receptive are clearly
delineated and experienced. This conflict helps
birth or rebirth the ego. Colors tend to be very
bright in mandalas of this stage.

PLATE 9
Mandalas early in the Great Round are diffuse,
suggesting myriad tiny creatures thriving in a
liquid environment. This mandala is an example
of stage 2, Bliss, where soft colors are often used.

PLATE 10
As the cycle of growth is fulfilled in stage 9, Crystallization, there is a slowing of creative energy. Colors are often rich, autumnal. A sense of completion, of fulfillment, predominates.
(Drawing by Martha DeHart)

PLATE 11
As a cycle on the Great Round comes to an end, mandalas may appear chaotic. This is the necessary coming apart of stage 11, Fragmentation. Colors are often bright, even psychedelic.

PLATE 12

Color choices reflect something about you. For the artist who colored this mandala, black is a powerful, mysterious, and comforting color. The pastel colors represent spiritual insights, while deep pink symbolizes the artist's physical body.

PLATE 13

The bright background colors in this mandala give a sense of energy, expansiveness, and excitement. The blue wings suggest to this artist her calling to share her wisdom with others.

Mandalas for Coloring

Mandala 1

During Stage 0, Clear Light, the profound simplicity of an empty circle invites, shelters, brings focus, and gives form. The empty circle suggests potentials, defines a boundary, and establishes center and circumference. The circle is an image of God, of eternity, of union between the One and the many. It is the signature of the inner urge toward wholeness that Jung called the Self. Take a moment to ponder and discover what it means to you to enter the circle, to join this dance of the twelve stages of the Great Round and their mandala forms.

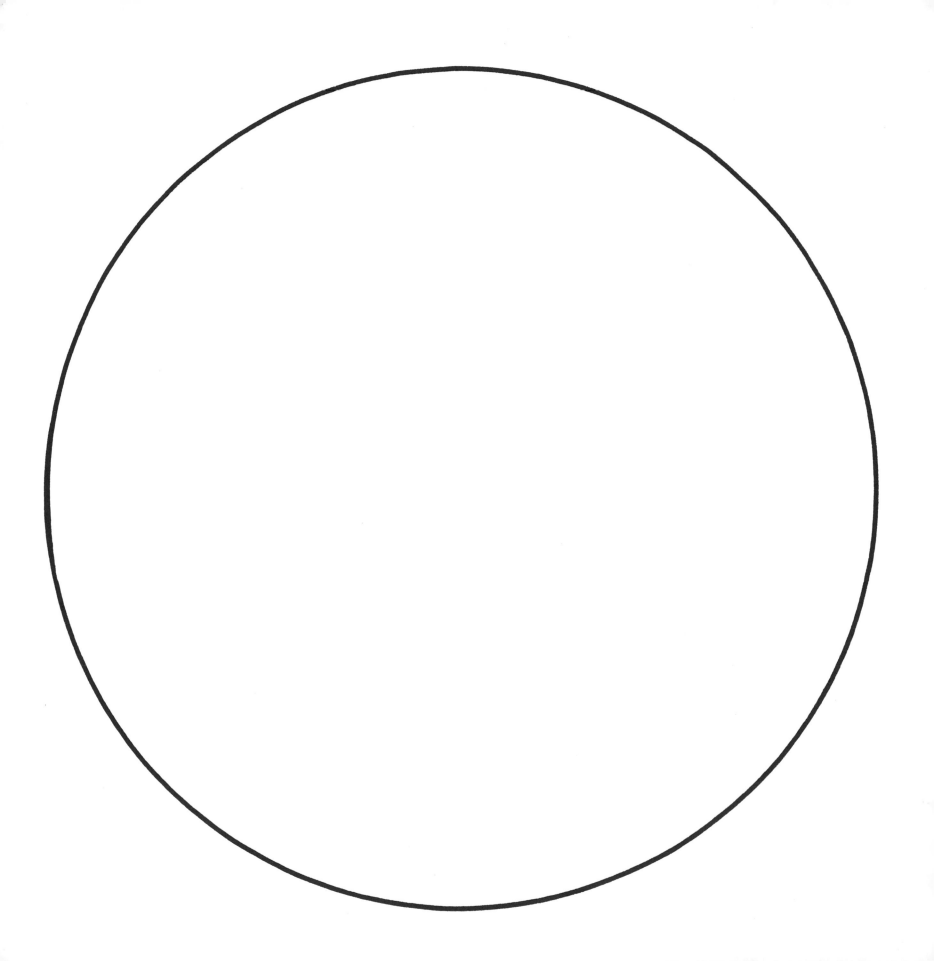

MANDALA 2

During stage 1, Void, you experience a moment beyond ordinary clock time, a dreamtime when your inner world is profoundly reordered. In the metaphorical language of spirituality, it is a time when spirit enters matter and takes the form you know as your body.

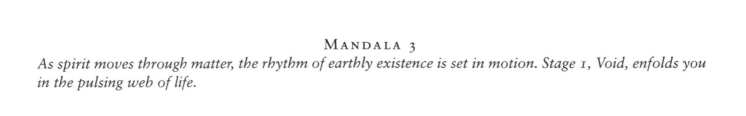

MANDALA 3

As spirit moves through matter, the rhythm of earthly existence is set in motion. Stage 1, Void, enfolds you in the pulsing web of life.

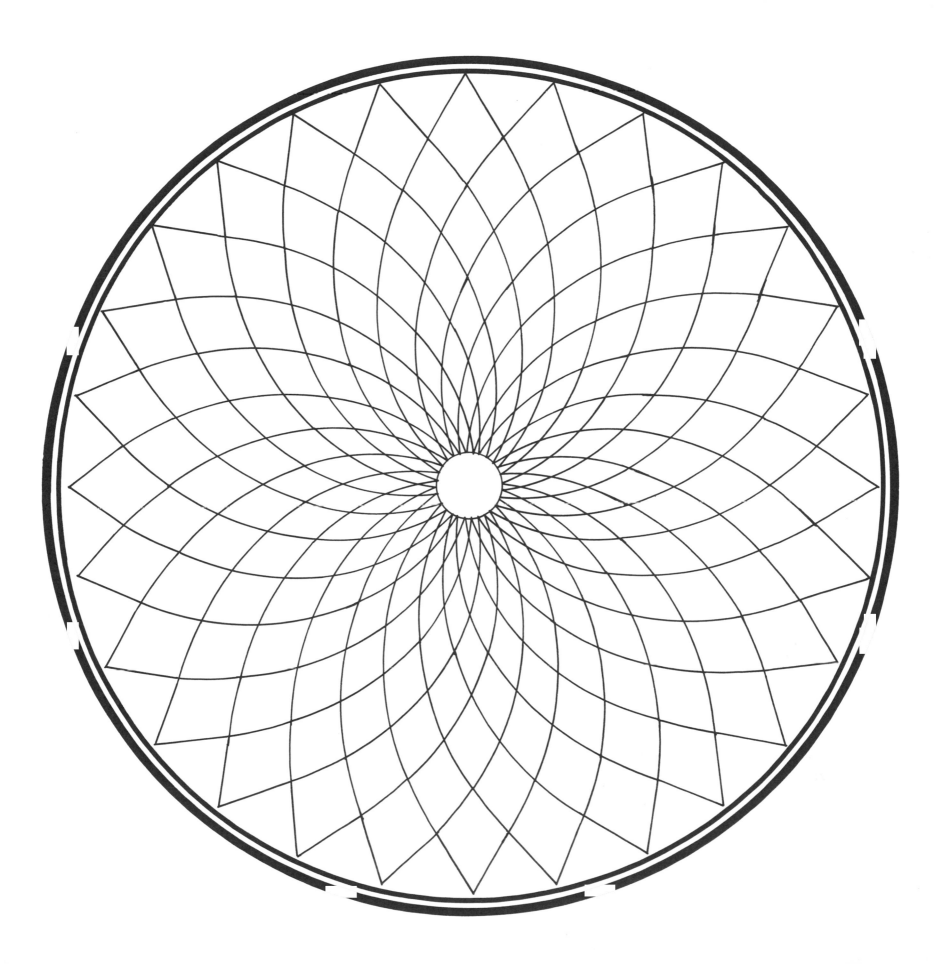

MANDALA 4

During stage 1, Void, the consciousness that holds all possibilities and potentials in seamless unity, separates into the dualities familiar to you in your daily thoughts: yes/no, good/bad, I/not-I. Thus the One becomes the many.

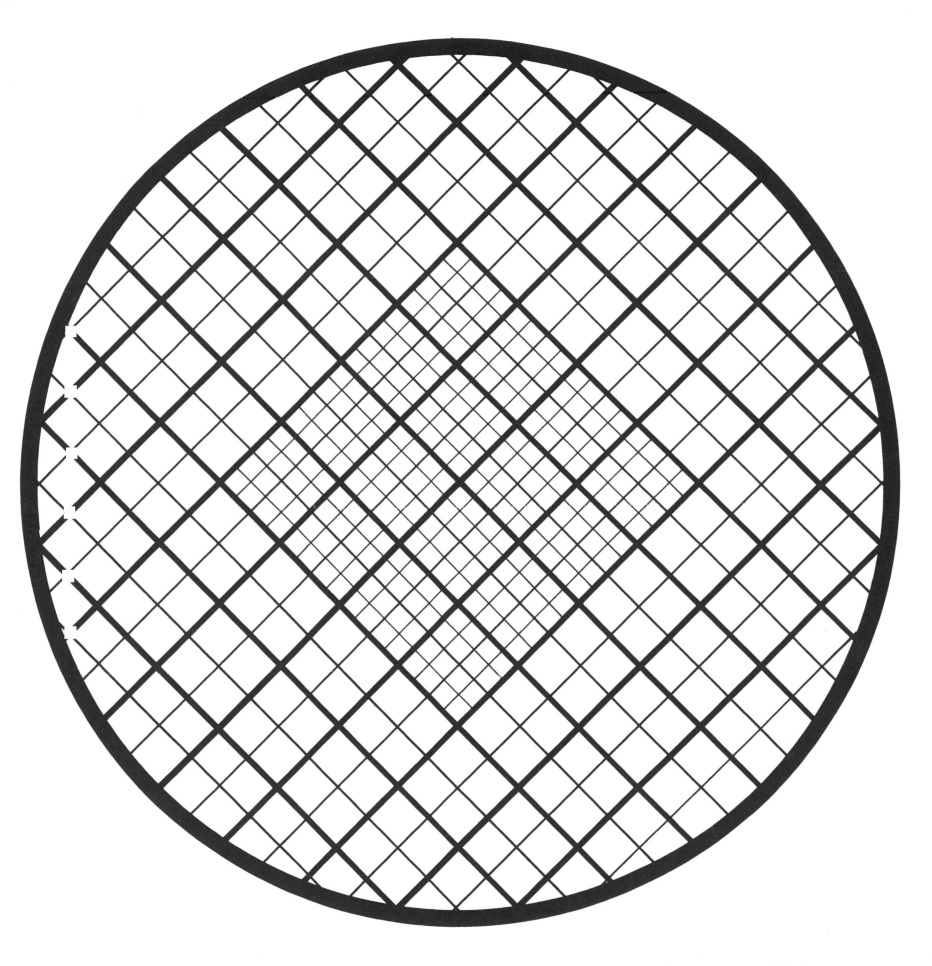

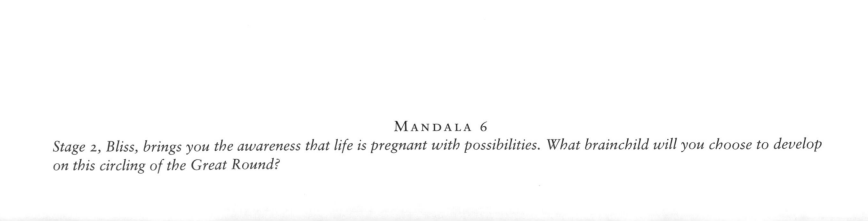

MANDALA 6

Stage 2, Bliss, brings you the awareness that life is pregnant with possibilities. What brainchild will you choose to develop on this circling of the Great Round?

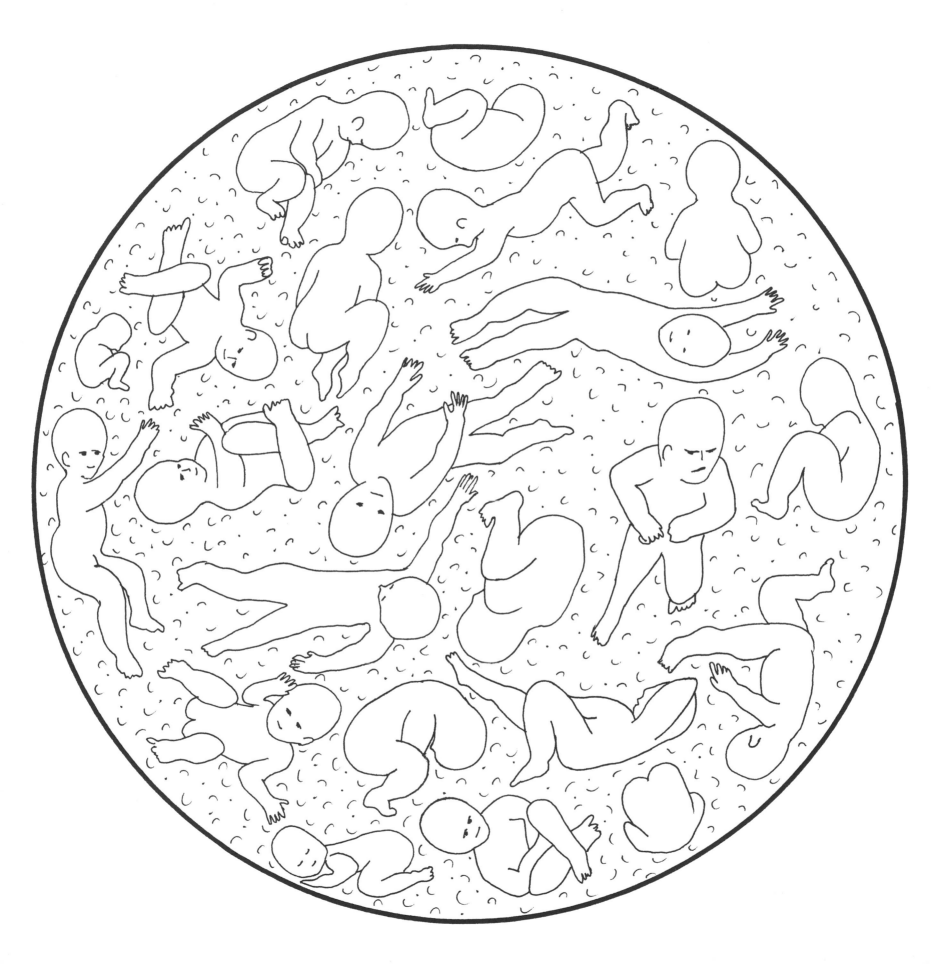

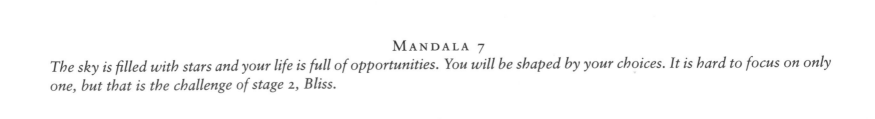

MANDALA 7

The sky is filled with stars and your life is full of opportunities. You will be shaped by your choices. It is hard to focus on only one, but that is the challenge of stage 2, Bliss.

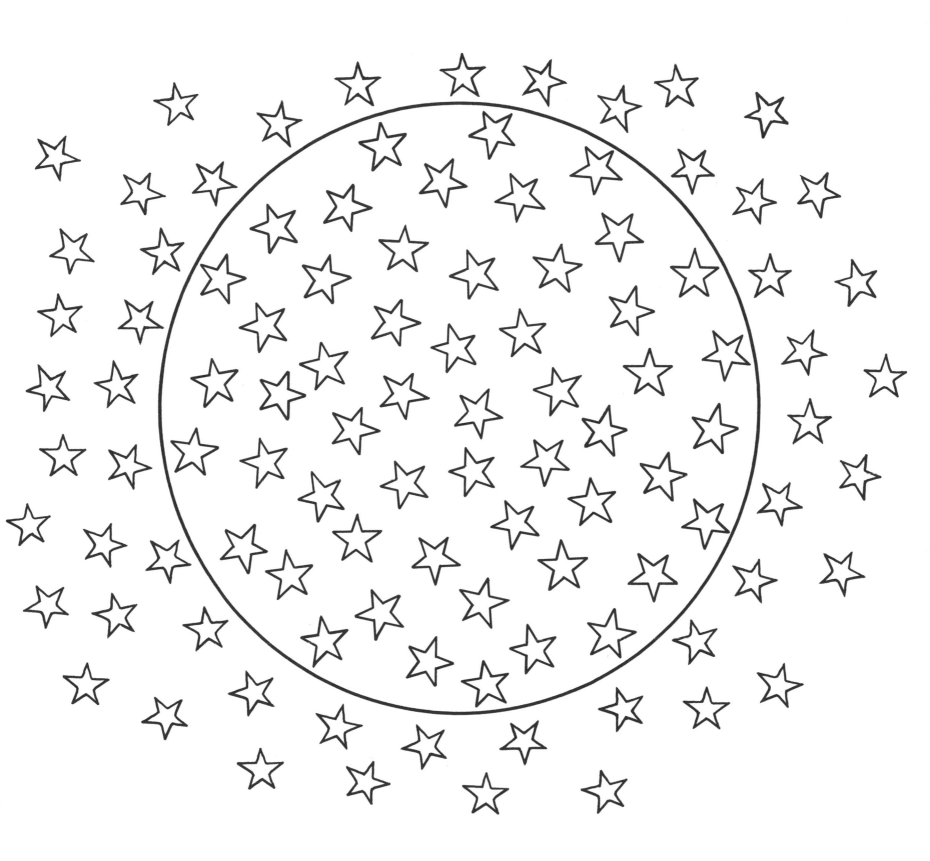

MANDALA 8

Your experience of stage 2, Bliss, resonates with your earliest memories from birth or even before. The mystery of new life is celebrated in mandalas such as this one signifying the regenerative powers of the Mother Goddess, whom ancients worshiped as the source of life. (After an illustration in Marija Gimbutas, The Language of the Goddess*)*

MANDALA 10

Is it a shoal of fish? The spinning of the wind? Or a fetus nestling in its mother's womb? Spiraling motion suggests the movement from the Center as we spin ourselves into being during stage 3, Labyrinth.

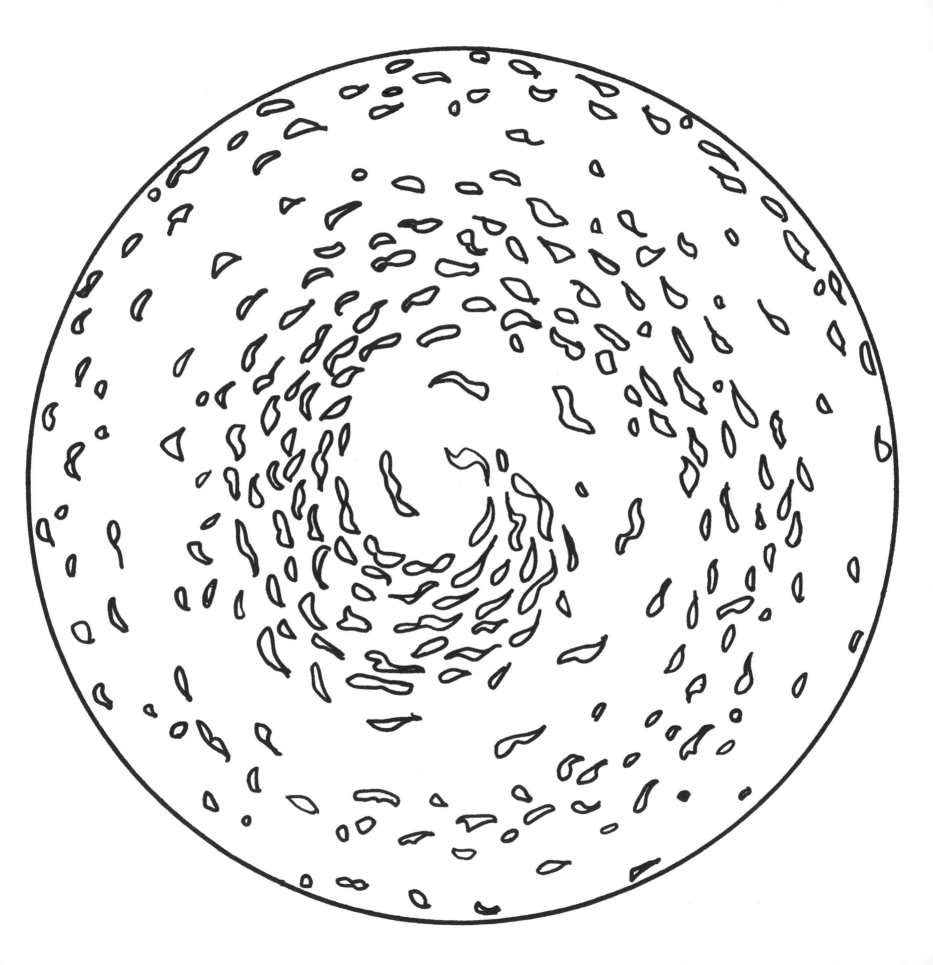

MANDALA 11

As you experience stage 3, Labyrinth, you may feel that you have begun an important journey, though where your journey is leading you remains unknown. There is excitement, a sense of expectancy, and anticipation as the path opens before you.

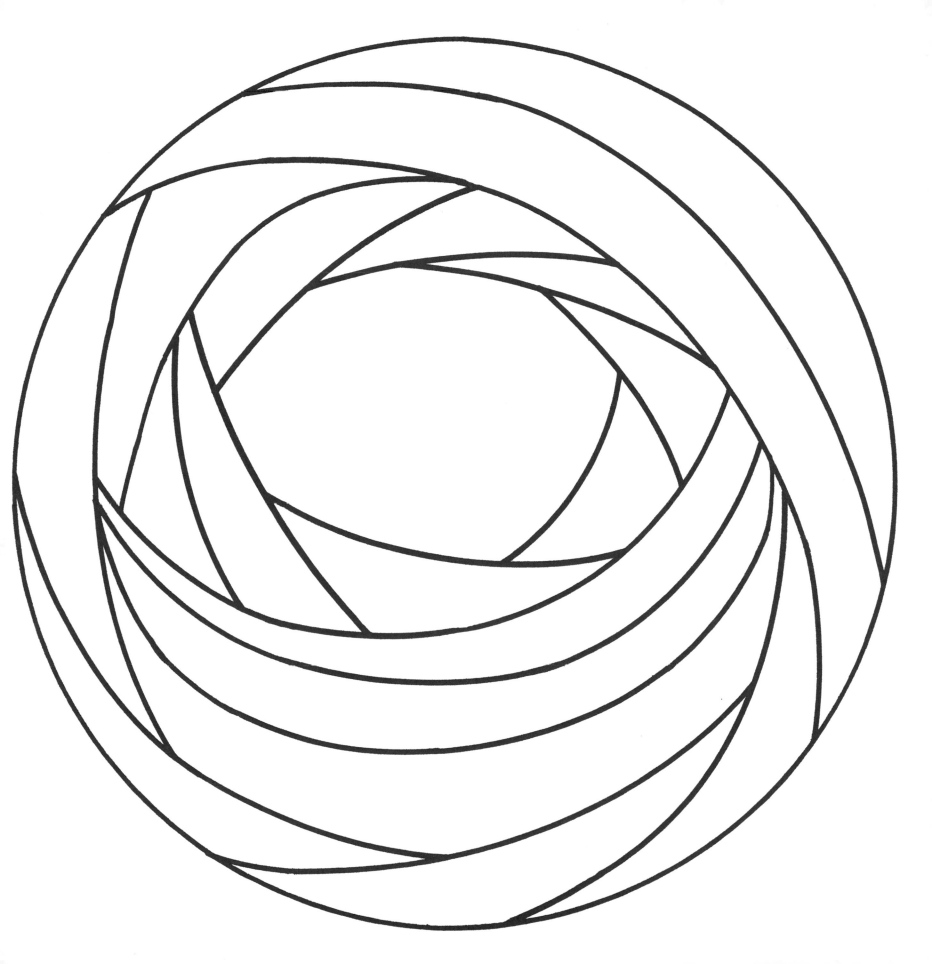

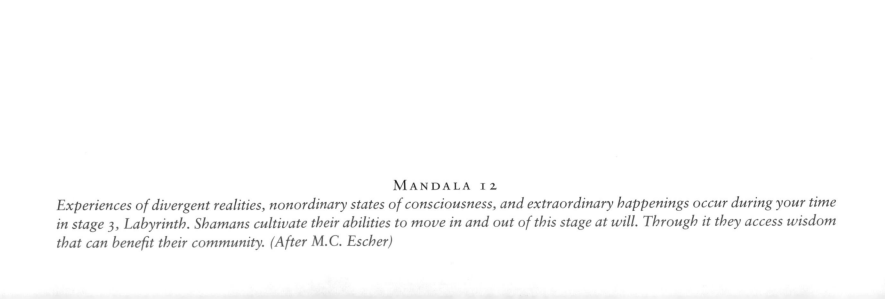

MANDALA 12

Experiences of divergent realities, nonordinary states of consciousness, and extraordinary happenings occur during your time in stage 3, Labyrinth. Shamans cultivate their abilities to move in and out of this stage at will. Through it they access wisdom that can benefit their community. (After M.C. Escher)

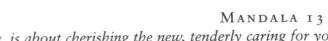

MANDALA 13

Stage 4, Beginning, is about cherishing the new, tenderly caring for your young inner self, or nurturing that brainchild singled out from the many available to you in stage 2, Bliss. It is as if you are pregnant with your self. Treat yourself gently.

During stage 4, Beginning, you are producing something new, even though its final form cannot yet be seen. This simple mandala design is found on the walls of a birthing chamber in an ancient palace on the island of Crete. Archeologists suggest that it may represent the cervix. You can use the dot as a beginning point for your own design. Perhaps it will reflect something you are "birthing." (After an illustration in Marija Gimbutas, The Language of the Goddess*)*

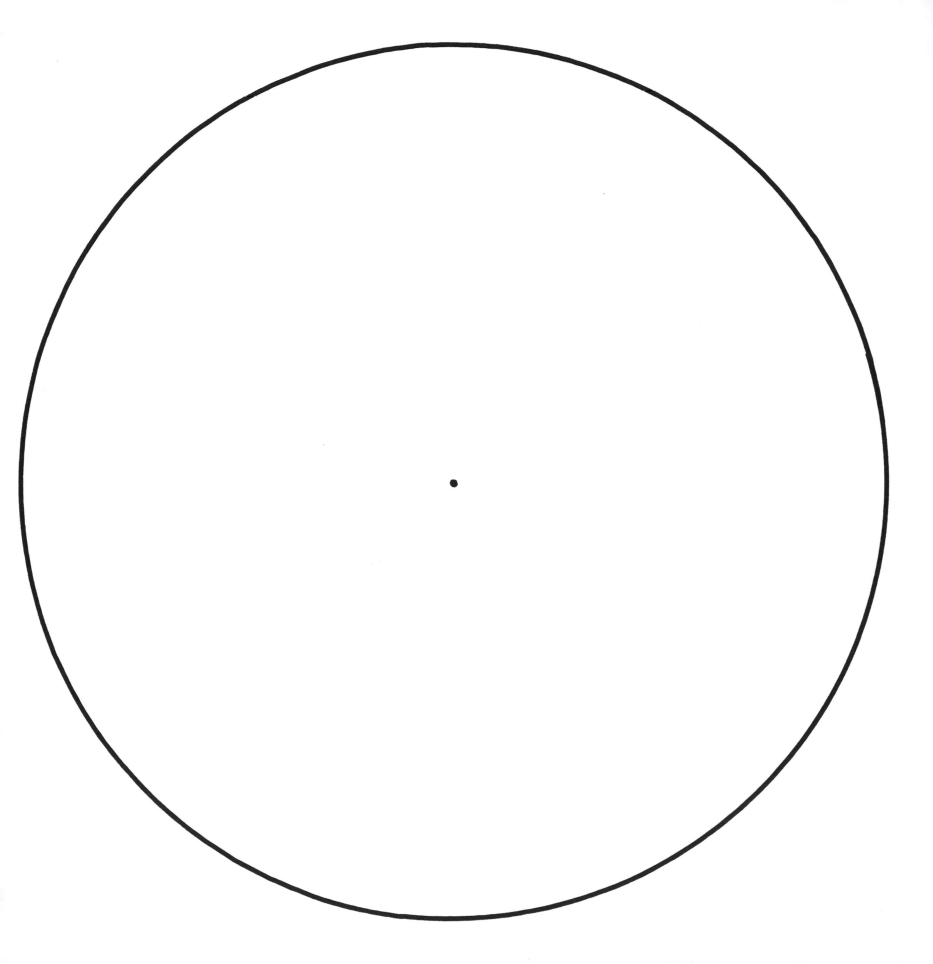

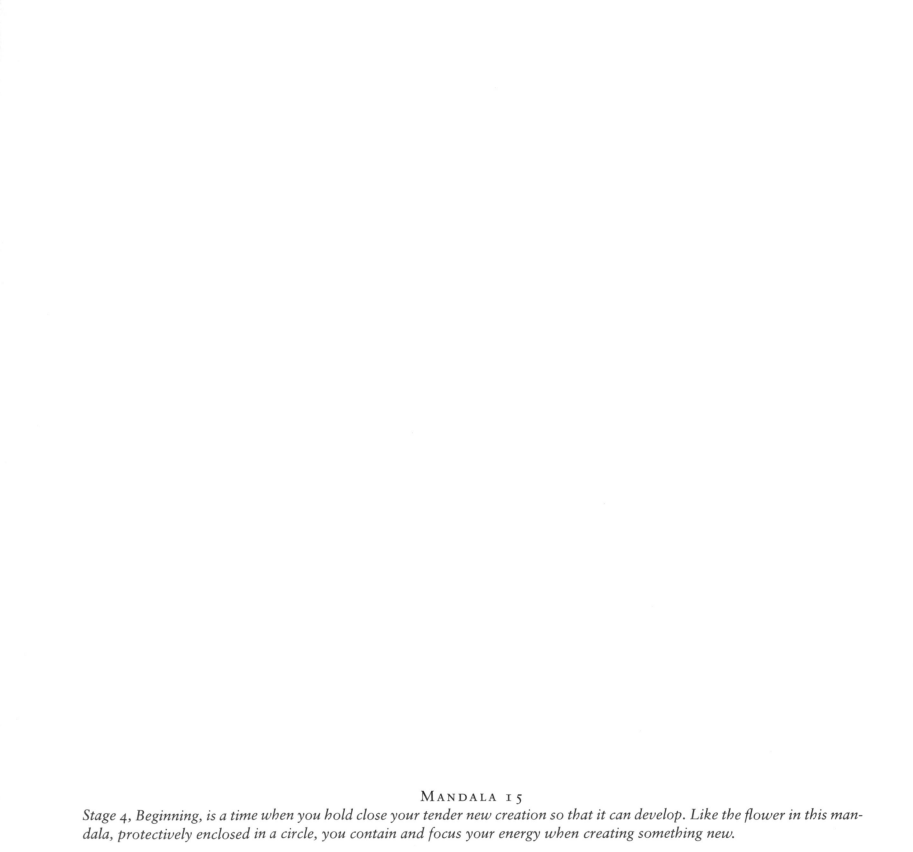

MANDALA 15

Stage 4, Beginning, is a time when you hold close your tender new creation so that it can develop. Like the flower in this mandala, protectively enclosed in a circle, you contain and focus your energy when creating something new.

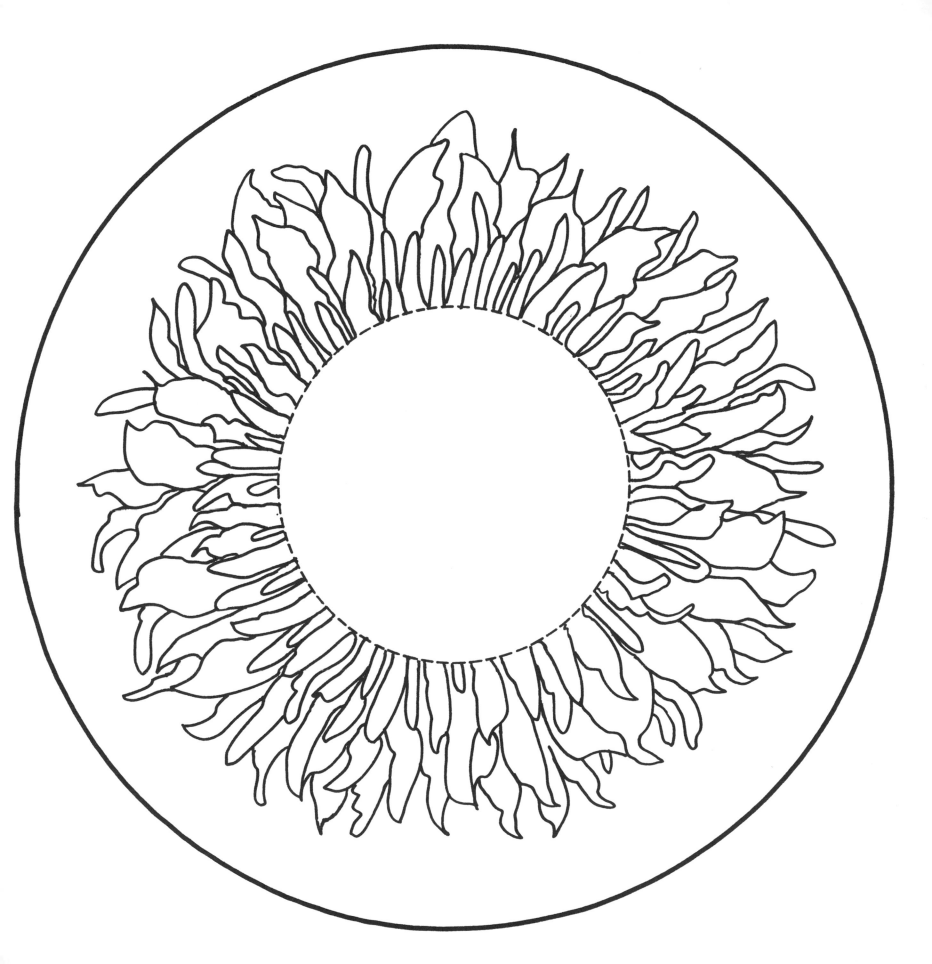

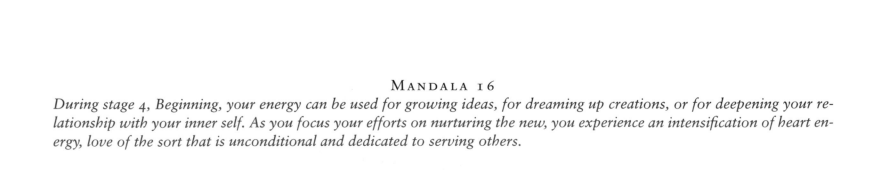

MANDALA 16

During stage 4, Beginning, your energy can be used for growing ideas, for dreaming up creations, or for deepening your relationship with your inner self. As you focus your efforts on nurturing the new, you experience an intensification of heart energy, love of the sort that is unconditional and dedicated to serving others.

MANDALA 17

During stage 5, Target, you experience a sense of urgency as you encounter limits that seem to block your progress. You may feel angry, scared, or confused. This mandala can be used to explore your feelings.

Inner circle: Name or draw those things that you fear most. Fill in the ring around the circle with a color that represents courage.

Second circle: Name or draw teachers, guides, and mentors, living or of the spirit world.

Third circle: Name or draw the negative thoughts and behaviors that arise from your fears.

Fourth circle: Name or draw positive behaviors that help you manage your fear.

Fifth circle: Write affirmations that address your fears. Read these aloud.

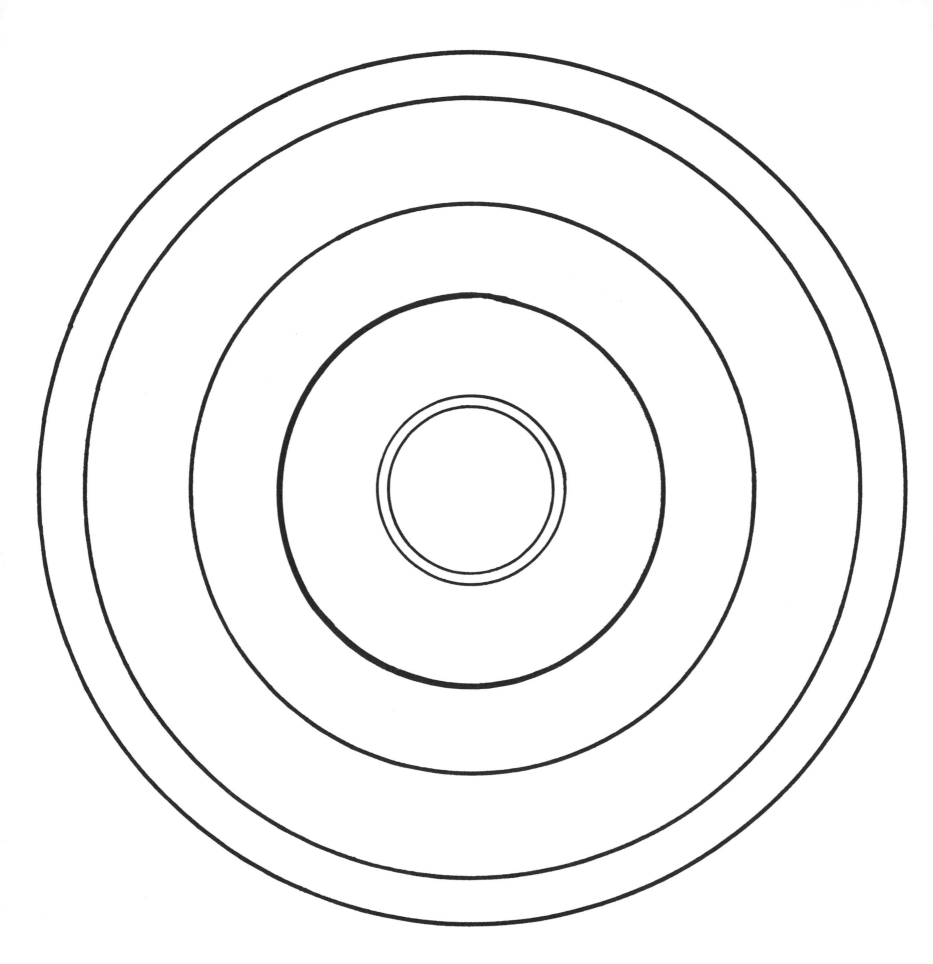

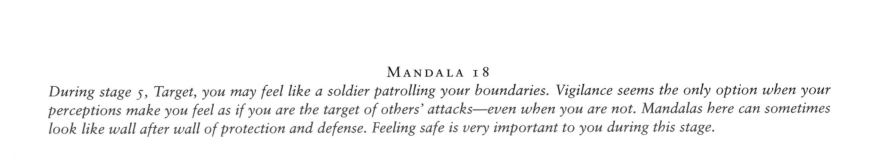

MANDALA 18

During stage 5, Target, you may feel like a soldier patrolling your boundaries. Vigilance seems the only option when your perceptions make you feel as if you are the target of others' attacks—even when you are not. Mandalas here can sometimes look like wall after wall of protection and defense. Feeling safe is very important to you during this stage.

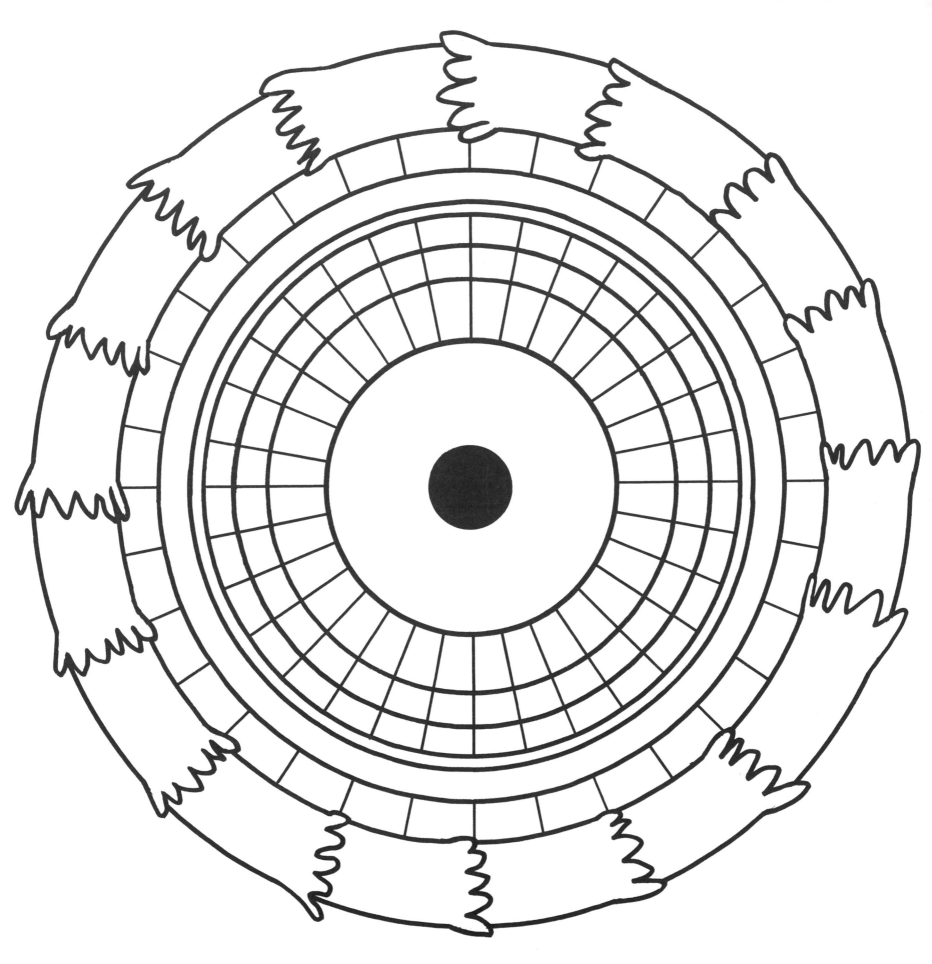

MANDALA 19

Personal habits and other rituals help you feel safe during stage 5, Target, when emotions intensify. Like the strong walls of a castle sheltering a garden within, this Celtic mandala has mazelike bands of designs protecting tender leafy vines in the center.

Mystics transcend the emotional intensity of stage 5, Target. They use the target mandala form to communicate their insights and experiences. This mandala depicts Hildegard of Bingen's vision of all beings together, dancing, singing, and celebrating God's creation. Nine circles of angels and human beings surround an empty circle representing "the mystery of the center where beauty is born." (Matthew Fox, Illuminations of Hildegard of Bingen, *p. 77)*

MANDALA 21

Stage 6, Dragon Fight, brings about the polarization of the opposites in our lives: dark/light, male/female, angel/devil. The increased inner conflict creates energy that can be channeled into the expansion of consciousness. (After M. C. Escher)

When you endure the tension of the opposites during stage 6, Dragon Fight, a new viewpoint eventually emerges that transcends and resolves the conflict. So we see in this mandala the opposites of mother earth and father sky, male and female energy. The sun rising between the earth and sky signifies the new element appearing. Like the child that inherits qualities from both parents but is identical with neither, the solution to conflicts brings something entirely new to the situation.

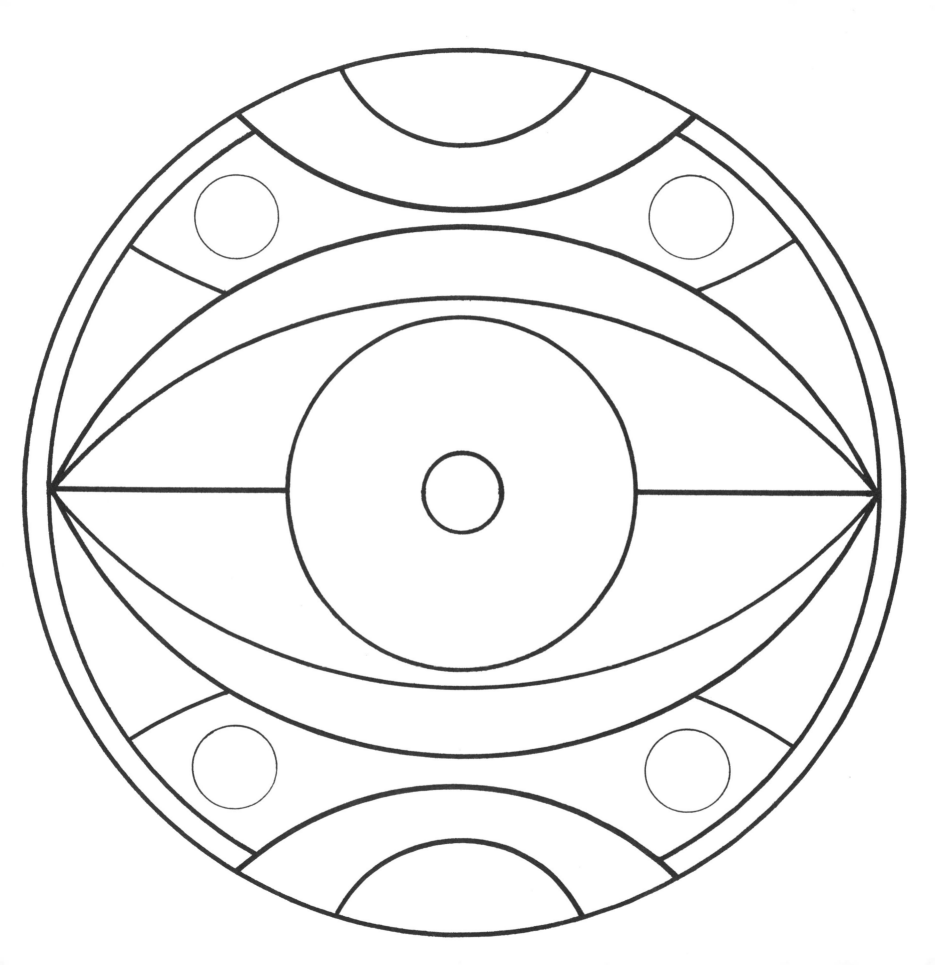

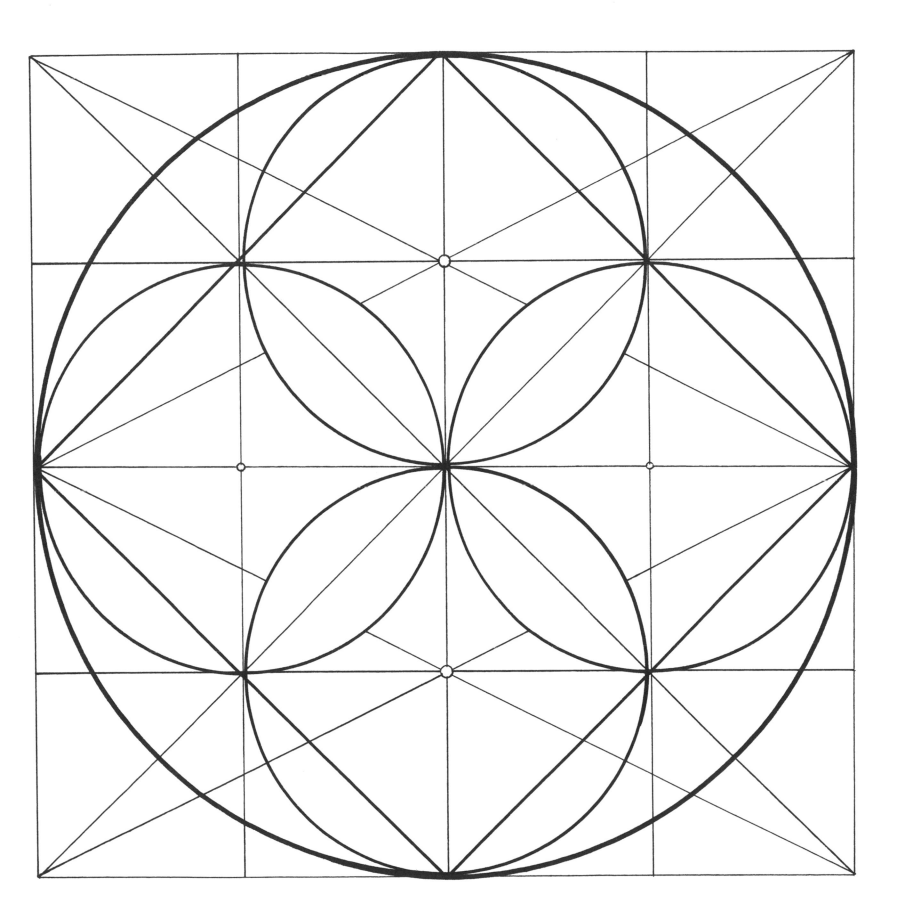

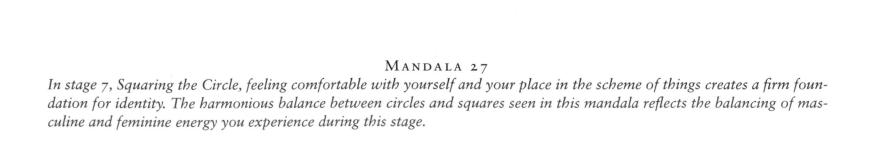

MANDALA 27

In stage 7, Squaring the Circle, feeling comfortable with yourself and your place in the scheme of things creates a firm foundation for identity. The harmonious balance between circles and squares seen in this mandala reflects the balancing of masculine and feminine energy you experience during this stage.

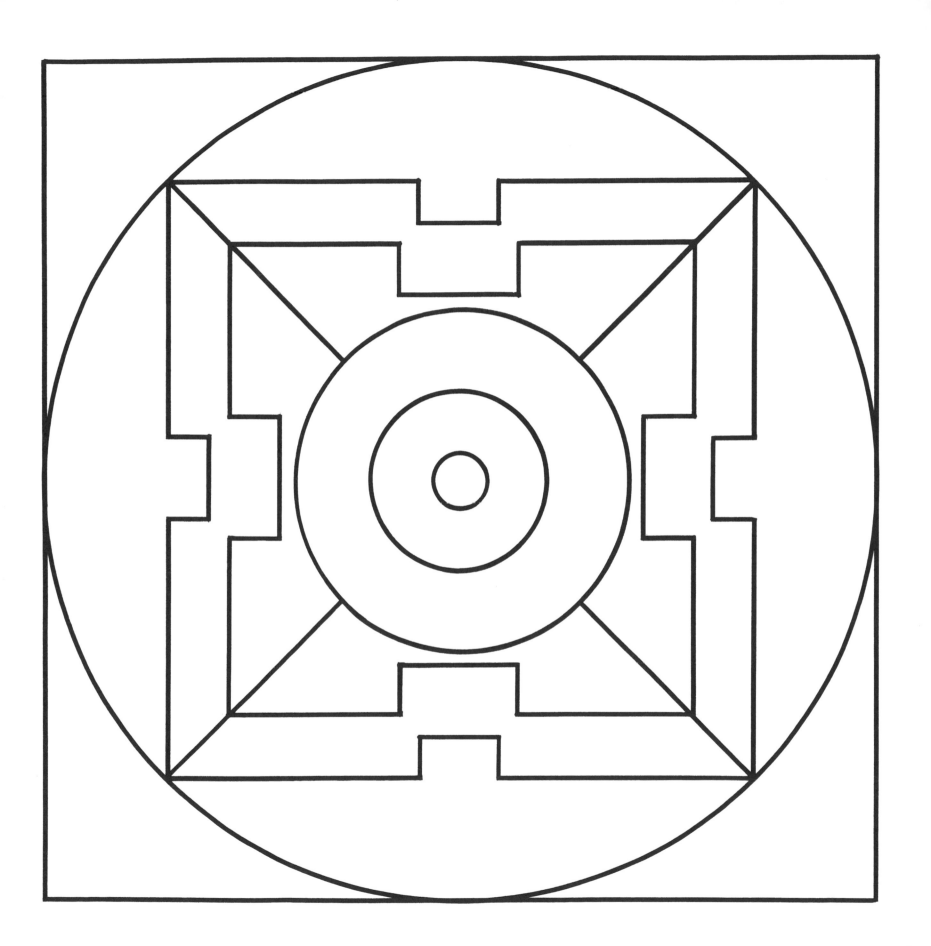

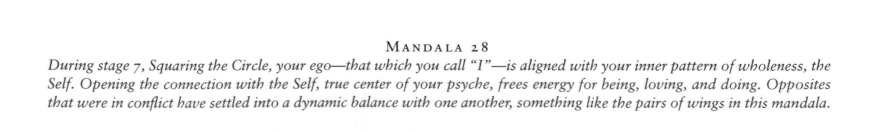

MANDALA 28

During stage 7, Squaring the Circle, your ego—that which you call "I"—is aligned with your inner pattern of wholeness, the Self. Opening the connection with the Self, true center of your psyche, frees energy for being, loving, and doing. Opposites that were in conflict have settled into a dynamic balance with one another, something like the pairs of wings in this mandala.

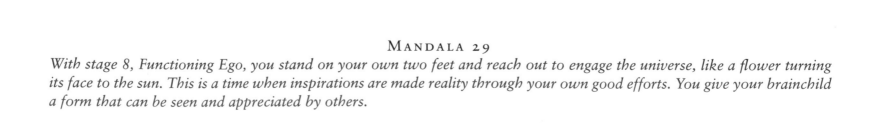

MANDALA 29

With stage 8, Functioning Ego, you stand on your own two feet and reach out to engage the universe, like a flower turning its face to the sun. This is a time when inspirations are made reality through your own good efforts. You give your brainchild a form that can be seen and appreciated by others.

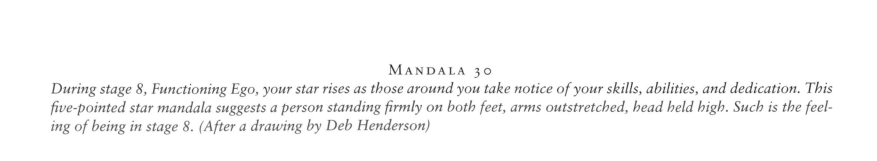

MANDALA 30

During stage 8, Functioning Ego, your star rises as those around you take notice of your skills, abilities, and dedication. This five-pointed star mandala suggests a person standing firmly on both feet, arms outstretched, head held high. Such is the feeling of being in stage 8. (After a drawing by Deb Henderson)

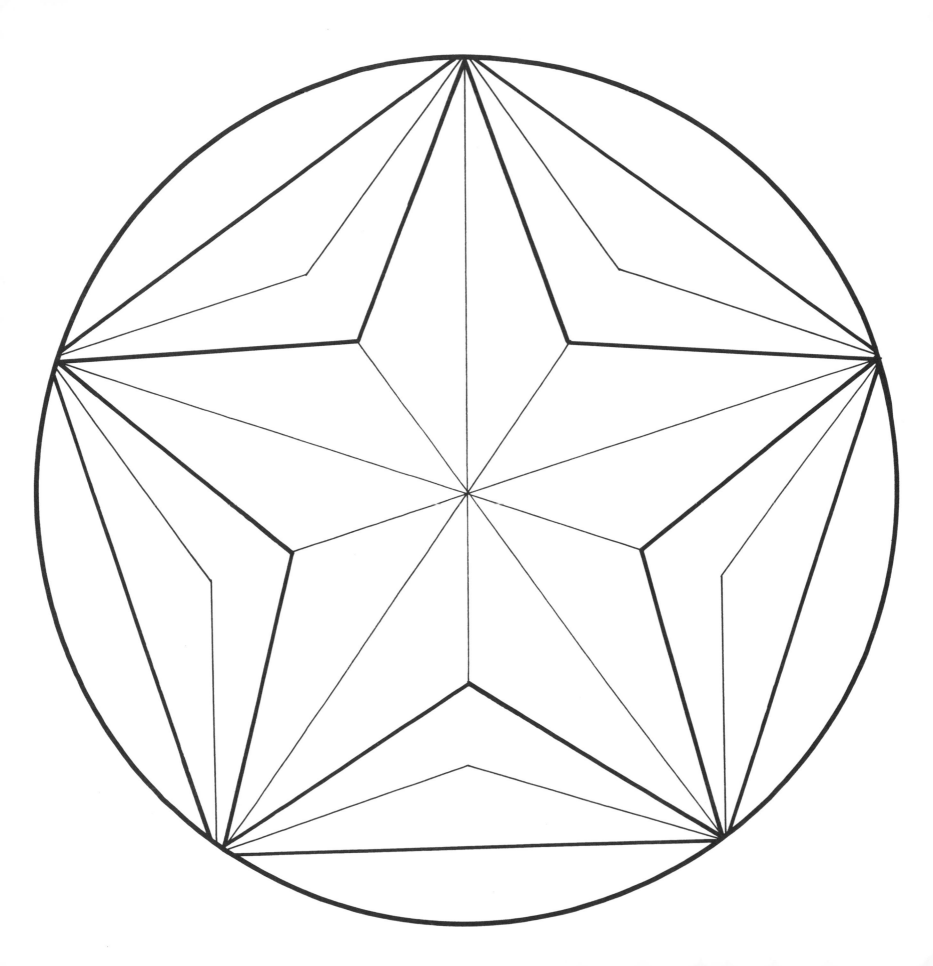

During stage 8, Functioning Ego, you work comfortably within a group or alone as needed to accomplish your goals. You may amaze even yourself at all that is taking shape through your hands. In this Native American mandala, the static cross form sprouts wings and becomes a spinning swastika, ancient symbol of the sun. The movement in this design reflects the active doing that exemplifies this stage. (After an illustration in Franz Boas, Primitive Art)

MANDALA 32

During stage 8, Functioning Ego, you reach out to touch, to take hold of life, to create new and wondrous things. Let your imagination give meaning to the five circles in this mandala. Do they represent the aspects of a complex project you are working on? Are they people with whom you seek to cooperate to accomplish your goals? Or are they reminders of the waxing phases of the moon and awareness of the need to work in harmony with the laws of nature?

MANDALA 33

With stage 9, Crystallization, your work takes its final form. Surveying your labor of love, you find deep satisfaction in what you have accomplished. In this dynamic mandala, based on the number six, the interplay of lines brings one circle, then another, dancing into view. Just so, you review each facet of your creation and say to yourself, "This is good." (Based on a Hindu design signifying creation)

MANDALA 34

During stage 8, Crystallization, what were once scattered pieces of a puzzle have come together in harmony as you complete your task for this circling of the Great Round. An underlying structure based on the number eight imparts order to the complex elements of this mandala. Derived from a Turkish design, it communicates the Islamic belief that all is held within the One, or Allah.

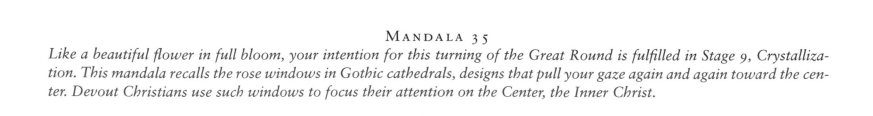

MANDALA 35

Like a beautiful flower in full bloom, your intention for this turning of the Great Round is fulfilled in Stage 9, Crystalliza-tion. This mandala recalls the rose windows in Gothic cathedrals, designs that pull your gaze again and again toward the cen-ter. Devout Christians use such windows to focus their attention on the Center, the Inner Christ.

During stage 9, Crystallization, you begin to see through the appearances of things to grasp the fundamental structures of reality. This mandala is based on the Sri Yantra, a sacred Hindu design used for meditation. The single downward-pointing triangle in the center is a symbol of divine feminine energy, the source of all creation. Expanding outward from the center, upward- and downward-pointing triangles signify all male and female creatures coming into being. Lotus petals enclose the field of emanation and lines that represent the four directions, the four elements, and other significant ordering principles border the whole. Because it is believed that the powers of the feminine are heightened during darkness, some practitioners recommend working with this yantra only during daylight hours.

Mandala 37

Stage 10, Gates of Death, marks the beginning of your disengagement from that which has held your attention for this circuit of the Great Round. This stage opens the equally important completion of the cycle that clears the way for a new beginning. You may feel compelled to turn your back on your accomplishments, to forgo security, or to let go of the way things have been, and step through a gateway to a mysterious unknown. This commences a journey downward, into the depths of yourself.

Stage 10, Gates of Death, brings you a sense of the relentless passage of time. The wheel of life turns on, sometimes up and sometimes down. Those caught up in their attachments try to hold back the sands of time. For others, willing to let go, all is as it should be.

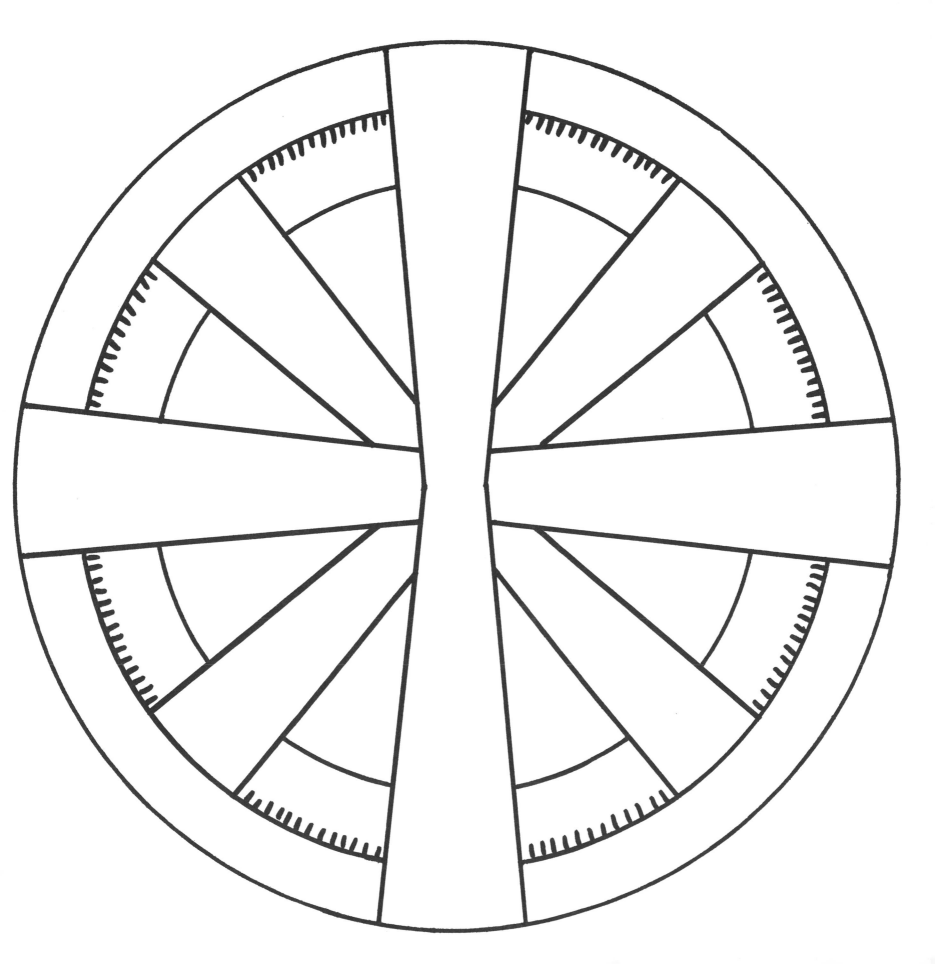

MANDALA 39

Stage 10, Gates of Death, requires a sacrifice. The parting with what was can feel like a bittersweet pause at a crossroads, an urgent summons into alien territory, or even the ultimate surrender of crucifixion. You are being separated from that which is no longer needed. Celtic crosses like the one in this mandala dot the landscape of Scotland. Tall, silent, enduring stone, they stand against the sky washed by the winds and rains of countless seasons, reminders that even though things change, there is a part of you that lives on.

During stage 10 , Gates of Death, you may begin to see that destruction opens the way for creation. As in this mandala, based on the Kali Yantra of Hinduism, both energies are ever present. The eight-petaled lotus represents the goddess Kali in her nurturing maternal aspect. The inner circle, traditionally colored black, reveals her also as Destroyer, the dark womb that eventually absorbs all into nonbeing. And the center triangle, the ultimate symbol of divine feminine creative energy, holds the pearly spark of new life.

MANDALA 41

During stage 11, Fragmentation, things come apart in your life. It is a time of increased confusion when you drop your groceries, the car won't start, your roof is leaking, and your power is cut off. It is the completion of the Great Round in a necessary period of chaos. Remember: to make an omelet, you must first break the eggs.

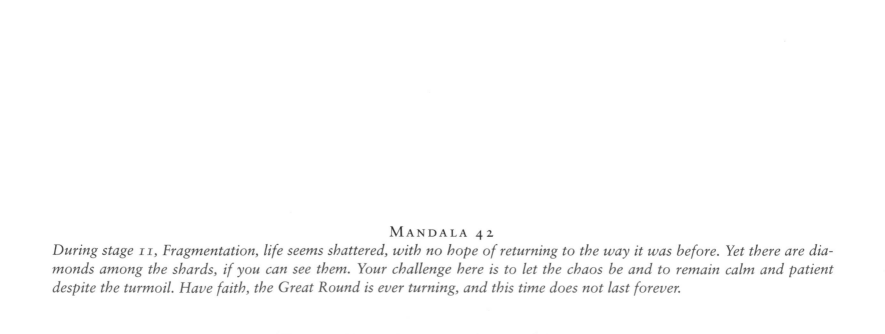

MANDALA 42

During stage 11, Fragmentation, life seems shattered, with no hope of returning to the way it was before. Yet there are diamonds among the shards, if you can see them. Your challenge here is to let the chaos be and to remain calm and patient despite the turmoil. Have faith, the Great Round is ever turning, and this time does not last forever.

During stage 11, Fragmentation, you feel lost, as if swallowed up in the belly of Jonah's whale. Like the killer whale depicted in this Native American design, you may feel your bones have been picked clean. All the better to become flexible, to learn to bend instead of breaking, to surrender to the shaping of spirit. (After an illustration in Franz Boas, Primitive Art*)*

MANDALA 44

During stage 11, Fragmentation, confusion comes about because the pattern is beyond your comprehension. As envisioned by Hildegard von Bingen, the experience can be "cleansing, purifying, and healing." This mandala is based on her vision of cosmic judgment when the elements of fire, water, and air break open and make the land move. "Lightning flashed and claps of thunder boomed. And everything that was mortal breathed out its life." This chaos precedes an accounting when those who have cherished the cosmos and imitated its ways of harmony will shine with an eternal light that comes from "the Lord of all things." When you know the rhythms of life and live in keeping with them you need not fear the ending of the cycle. (Quotations from Matthew Fox, Illuminations of Hildegard of Bingen, *pp. 107–8)*

MANDALA 45

During stage 12, Transcendent Ecstasy, you experience a shift from chaos to transformative wisdom, a reordering of all that was broken. This stage is a coming together of all that went before, a time of profound joy, when you feel perfectly in step with the cosmic dance. (After a drawing by Clara Klug)

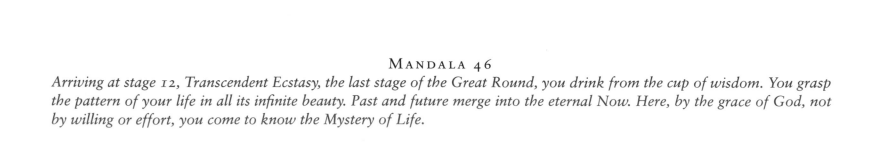

MANDALA 46

Arriving at stage 12, Transcendent Ecstasy, the last stage of the Great Round, you drink from the cup of wisdom. You grasp the pattern of your life in all its infinite beauty. Past and future merge into the eternal Now. Here, by the grace of God, not by willing or effort, you come to know the Mystery of Life.

Stage 12, Transcendent Ecstasy, is a moment of wholeness, of knowing rather than thinking. Mandalas such as this one signify the fruition of deep inner work through which you become aware that the true center of your psyche is the mysterious Self, that dynamic center Jung identified as an inner image of God. Pictured here is the lotus, a flowering plant that touches all four primal elements. Its roots are in the earth, its green growth is supported by water, its stalk ascends into the air, and its flower embraces the fiery sun. For Chinese mystics, the lotus is the mythic Golden Flower, symbol of the quest for enlightenment. (After an illustration in C. G. Jung, Mandala Symbolism*)*

MANDALA 48

During stage 12, Transcendent Ecstasy, all is in perfect balance, a peaceful ending to the stages of change that are the Great Round. Be still and open yourself to knowing the true center of yourself, the One, and rest in the knowledge of who you are. Soon enough you will move on to the dreamtime, Stage 1, Void, and a new beginning on the Great Round.